# Legal Research in England and Wales

**Revised Edition - August 1992**

**John Jeffries**

and

**Christine Miskin**



Guides to Legal Research: No 1

Series editor: Christine Miskin

Legal Information Resources Limited

1992

Printed and Published
by
Legal Information Resources Ltd
Elphin House, 1 New Road, Mytholmroyd,
Hebden Bridge, West Yorkshire HX7 5DZ

# ACKNOWLEDGMENTS

The Series Editor would like to acknowledge the help she has received over the years from both fellow law librarians and generations of trainee solicitors engaged in undertaking intractable problems for busy principals.

Gratitude is also expressed to Judith Barden, Lillian Stevenson Robert Logan and Janice Sayer who have read the text and offered helpful comments. Needless to say any errors remain the authors' responsibility.

# PREFACE

This guide is intended for those new, or relatively new, to legal research including trainee and newly qualified solicitors, and those studying the law. It describes the main source materials which are used by legal practitioners, and outlines the best ways of exploiting them.

It is important to recognise that legal research is an exercise in problem solving which depends upon finding the most cost and time effective method of working. The techniques best used in each piece of work will vary with the nature of the problem. There are no "right" approaches, but some are more efficient than others. This is a process of acquiring skills and you will become more skilled the more you practise. You cannot expect to learn the techniques of legal research by reading about them. You will acquire these techniques by using the source materials. This guide will show you where to start, and indicate some of the pitfalls to be avoided.

Worked examples of problems are included in the text to give further guidance. It is suggested that these will prove to be of most use if you can read through them in your own library with the relevant books to hand.

Other titles in this series will describe the materials used in more specialised areas of work. This guide does not cover European Communities law, although it is recognised that many English legal research problems will have an EC dimension. A sister publication deals with legal research and the law of the European Communities.

# CONTENTS

# Chapter 1: INTRODUCTION

## 1.1 Preparation

There are a number of ground rules which apply to researching any legal subject. It is a good idea to think about them at the outset of a piece of work.

### 1.1.1 The value of information

Almost any piece of information can be retrieved - at a price. Costs might arise because of the resources used in the search. Online charges are an obvious example, or it might be the cost of the labour of the person carrying out the work. Only the user of the information can determine whether the quest for information is worth the expenditure of time, effort and other resources. But that is only one side of the coin. What must also be weighed is the cost of doing without a piece of information. In many cases the true value of the information may be much greater than the actual cost of retrieving it.

### 1.1.2 Analysing the problem

It is important to establish the parameters of the research. What is the precise nature of the matter in question? A small amount of time spent thinking about the character of the current problem will probably pay dividends in terms of satisfactory results obtained in the most cost-effective manner.

First of all, think of the keywords which you would use to describe the problem and consider whether anyone writing about the subject would express themselves in similar terms. Can you identify "terms of art" - the expressions which are used exclusively to describe the phenomena in question? Failure to identify the correct terminology will result in wasted effort and inadequate results. Remember that synonyms and near synonyms abound in the English language. There are, moreover, homonyms - words with the same spelling but different meanings. And even a precise technical usage might occur in a number of entirely different contexts. For example, the term "restrictive covenant" appears in both conveyancing and employment contract literature. Or consider in how many different contexts the term "disclosure" could appear in legal literature.

Having explored the terminology to your satisfaction, begin to arrange these keywords into concepts. Put together the things which belong together for the purposes of your research. Having done this, decide what is the most important concept, and arrange the others in descending order of priority. For example, if you are investigating "rights to light" the most important factor is that you are dealing with real property, and secondly that you are looking into the question of easements. There is an eminently practical reason for doing this, which is that very many legal indexes are classified. This means that specific headings are arranged under more general headings in a tree structure. Thus, if you do not start at the right branch you will not get to the correct twig.

It is also valuable to separate the facts of a particular case from the legal principles involved and decide the relationship between the two. If we consider personal injury - the injury might have arisen because of a medical accident. The nature of the problem breaks down into four areas:

* the facts of the case, which might involve a doctor, a hospital or a surgical procedure;

* the legal issues involved in the case, such as negligence;

* the remedy sought, for example damages;

* the relationship between the parties in the case, such as doctor and patient.

A similar logic can be applied to almost any set of facts and it will assist in broadening or narrowing the nature of the research.

### 1.1.3 Lateral thinking

Judges will often "distinguish" rather than "overrule" a decision of a lower court. Lawyers tend to look for ways around a problem rather than trying to face it head on. Legal research can also involve taking a sideways look at the world.

It would be deceptive to suppose that legal research could always be an entirely logical process. Logic helps, but often it is not enough. Frequently, it is necessary to seek analogies, and to find relationships amongst what appear to be unrelated ideas. This is because the use of legal materials is essentially frenetic and involves going from one source to another and cross-referring between several. The use you make of one source will be informed by what you have discovered in another. Another reason for using a variety of sources is that they are all the work of human beings, and human beings - however careful - can and do make mistakes.

### 1.1.4 Structure of the literature

Although the research process is often chaotic and frustrating, the available sources usually have a structure. Sometimes, sources are designed specifically to be used in conjunction with one another. This is especially true of the quartet of works published by Butterworths: *Halsbury's Laws of England*; *Halsbury's Statutes*; *The Digest*; and *Halsbury's Statutory Instruments*. Between them, these four works provide a legal encyclopaedia; a statement of the statute law in force; a summary of case law and a statement of the delegated legislation in force. These four works are intended to be used together and cross refer to each other.

## 1.2. The range of sources

The range of sources available to the legal researcher today is perplexingly rich and varied. Legal research can no longer be confined to conventionally printed and published material but might also include material stored in remote electronic databases; optical media searched by a microcomputer; floppy disks; official press releases and grey literature - the working documentation of organisations of various kinds including governmental and international non-governmental organisations. One might also coin the term "glossy literature" - usually free publications of professional firms, especially accountants, which are frequently invaluable.

### 1.2.1 Primary materials

Statutes, statutory instruments and case law are the bones of legal literature. Without these sources it can scarcely be said that the law could exist at all, because law has to be written down. Primary materials are usually published by official bodies like HMSO or semi-official bodies like the Incorporated Council of Law

Reporting. There has also been a longstanding role for commercial publishers.

As the practice of law has become more specialised, so an increasing range of specialised works has appeared which often reprint the primary materials applicable to an area of law with an expert commentary. These usually appear as looseleaf encyclopaedias and examples are *Encyclopaedia of Planning Law* and *Mahaffy and Dodson, Road Traffic Encyclopaedia*.

### 1.2.2 Student books, textbooks, and practitioners' books

It is becoming increasingly difficult to draw a distinction between the various publications of commercial law publishers. It is evident that some books are designed for the mass student market; some are intended to be a general almost philosophical statement of the law in a certain area and others are stores of practical "legal know-how". It is this last category of practitioner's books which are most useful in law firms. Generally speaking, experienced practitioners in those areas of work would know most of what they contain, but such books are one of the chief means by which comparative new-comers increase their knowledge. As an example of the different types of textbook available, in the field of contract *Chitty's Law of Contracts* is the major practitioner's work, whilst *Cheshire and Fifoot's Law of Contract* and *Treitel's Law of Contract* are students' texts and Lewison's *Interpretation of Contracts* is a philosophical work.

### 1.2.3 Journals

Legal journals contain much material of value to the practitioner including notes of recent cases, commentaries on significant cases and articles of current interest. Tracing a relevant article may often prove to be the most efficient means of initiating a piece of research.

### 1.2.4 Government information

Much material will have appeared in official publications before a Bill finally reaches the statute book. In the case of a major piece of legislation there are likely to have been Consultative Documents and a White Paper, press releases and all manner of working documents. It is essential to consider the range of materials associated with legislation in the pipeline when advising a client, as well as those which state the law as it stands on a given date. Ministerial circulars may have a significant bearing on the matter in hand. Many government reports such as those of the Monopolies and Mergers Commission, will be essential to the work of a commercial lawyer. There is an increasing volume of government information which affects legal practice. The *House of Commons Weekly Information Bulletin* can be consulted for details of the progress of current legislation. HMSO issues a series of daily, monthly and annual catalogues of its publications. Your librarian should also be able to help you track down government publications.

### 1.2.5 Non-legal sources

From time to time, it will become apparent to you that there does not seem to be very much law in a particular subject area. Or perhaps it looks as though material emanating from non-legal sources is of as much, or possibly greater, value than the black letter law itself. As with government information, you will need to turn to a wider range of sources to carry out effective legal research. One need only consider the range of bodies issuing codes and rule books in the financial sector. In the United Kingdom there are some 340 professional bodies and trade associations which publish various codes of conduct, ethics and practice. It would be impossible to enumerate all the sources which might provide material of value during the conduct of legal research.

It should not be forgotten that research is no longer exclusively a library or desk based process. If you need to telephone someone to obtain the information you need, then that is exactly what you should do.

### 1.2.6 Electronic information

Legal practice is making increasing demands on information technology for a wide variety of applications. There are a number of benefits to be derived from using information in electronic form. When remote databases are searched, the user pays only for the information actually used. You have access to a far wider range of materials than could be afforded by only the very largest research libraries and you have the opportunity to search in a more sophisticated manner. Information published in electronic form should be far more up-to-date than conventionally published sources.

Remote databases like LEXIS, JUSTIS and LAWTEL can be searched from an individual microcomputer or other terminal via a telecommunications link. In the case of LEXIS, the host computer is actually located in Dayton, Ohio.

The increasing range of products which are available in optical media like CD-ROM (compact disk read only memory) will have further implications for the publishing industry and might even replace some looseleaf services and other conventionally published works.

To access such highly sophisticated services requires a degree of sophistication in use. Training is needed, but it is also essential to have a search strategy. As with driving a car, the basic use of the controls needs to be second nature. The intellectual effort involved in online searching is analogous to road sense and route knowledge. To explore this further, you will need the training provided by database hosts and the manuals which accompany these various services. However, if you require a one-off search, your librarian should be able to help you.

## WORKS MENTIONED

*Halsbury's Laws of England 4th ed*
London, Butterworths, 1973-
56 vols
Annual and Cumulative Supplements
Index 1990

*Halsbury's Statutes 4th ed*
London, Butterworths, 1985-
50 vols
Current Statutes Service
Annual and Cumulative Supplements
Table of Statutes and General Index
Index 1991-92

*Halsbury's Statutory Instruments*
London, Butterworths
24 vols
Continually updated.
Black Volumes being replaced by Grey Volumes
Consolidated Index 1991-92

*The Digest: annotated British, Commonwealth and European Cases 3rd ed*
London, Butterworths, 1971-
51 vols
Continuation Volumes
Cumulative Supplement
Consolidated Table of Cases
Consolidated Index

*Encyclopaedia of Planning Law*
London, Sweet & Maxwell
Looseleaf

Mahaffy and Dodson
***Road traffic encyclopaedia.*** 3rd ed.
London, Butterworths
Looseleaf

*House of Commons Weekly Information Bulletin*
H.M.S.O.

*Daily List of Government Publications*
H.M.S.O.

*Monthly Catalogue of Government Publications*
H.M.S.O.

*Annual Catalogue of Government Publications*
H.M.S.O.

Cheshire and Fifoot
***Law of contract***. 12th ed.
London, Butterworths, 1991

Chitty
***On contracts***. 26th ed.
London, Sweet & Maxwell, 1989
2 vols

Lewison, K.
***Interpretation of contracts***
London, Sweet & Maxwell, 1989

Treitel, G.
***Law of contract***. 8th ed.
London, Sweet & Maxwell, 1991

# Chapter 2: BOOKS AND JOURNALS

## 2.1 Books

It is always worth trying to establish what books have been published in the area of your research. In a reasonably sized library quite complex problems can be surprisingly quickly resolved using commercially published books, because England and Wales supports such a high volume of law book publication. Reliance on books is safest in those areas of the law which change relatively slowly. Even when the law changes more rapidly, the publication of looseleaf works makes it relatively easy for you to update your knowledge. Unfortunately even with the opportunity provided by looseleaf publication, the updating cycle has more to do with economics than the convenience of the user, and you can still sometimes be misled by out of date information. Always take care that you are consulting the latest edition of a work and take note of the date at which the information was current. Never forget updating supplements etc where they exist.

To find out about books available on a particular topic, consult *Lawyers Law Books*, the latest publishers' catalogues and your library catalogue. One of the best available publishers' catalogues is the *Hammicks Bookshop Catalogue* which lists books in print by subject. Sweet and Maxwell and Butterworths produce annual catalogues, as do all the other major legal publishers.

There are also some specialist bibliographies available on specific subject areas such as labour law. These are listed in the relevant section of *Lawyers Law Books*. Several legal journals also contain regular comprehensive bibliographies. Examples are the *Journal of Energy and Natural Resources Law* and the *International Journal of Estuarine and Coastal Law.*

## 2.2 Journals

Journals provide a useful alternative source of current information on a topic. It is no longer necessary to scan large numbers of journals or to rely on the annual index which might accompany a title. There are a number of bibliographic works available to help you, as well as some electronic sources, the more important and generally accessible of which are described below.

### i. LEGAL JOURNALS INDEX

This index, which commenced publication in 1986, covers all legal journals published in the United Kingdom. It is the single most comprehensive source relating to current British legal periodical literature, recording more than a thousand items each month. It is published monthly and cumulates quarterly and annually.

There are in fact five indexes in this work:

- a detailed subject index with specific keywords assigned to each article of a page or more in length. The keywords are rotated alphabetically so that the same article may be traced by looking under any of the keywords assigned;
- an author index;

- an index to case comments or cases that have been the main topic of an article or comment;
- an index to legislation, and in particular to the specific sections of statutes that have been the main topic of an article or comment;
- a book review index;

It is also possible to request Legal Information Resources to search the electronic database used to generate the printed index. As well as saving labour, database searches can be executed in a far more sophisticated manner than is possible with a manual search, because of the nature of the thesaurus which controls the indexing vocabulary.

Some firms are able to search this index in electronic form.

### ii. CURRENT LAW

Major articles from a selection of British journals are indexed each month at the end of the appropriate subject heading. A cumulative list of articles arranged by subject appears at the end of each *Current Law Yearbook*. It should be remembered that this source is highly selective, and the subject headings themselves very general, but prior to 1986 it was the major British source.

### iii. LAWTEL

Like *Current Law*, LAWTEL indexes some journal articles, but this is a source where you may chance upon an article of significance when searching generally by subject.

### iv. LEXIS

LEXIS has the full text of the *New Law Journal* and *The Law Society's Gazette* from January 1986, plus *The Estates Gazette* from January 1991 and the *Journal of the Law Society of Scotland* from January 1990.

### v. CURRENT LAW INDEX (UNITED STATES)

This indexes most US but also some English legal periodicals. It has appeared monthly since 1980, and is partly cumulative. It is available as an online bibliographic database, spun on Lockheed Dialog, where it is called *Legal Resource Index*. It is also available as a videodisc in North America.

### vi. INDEX TO LEGAL PERIODICALS (UNITED STATES)

This is a similar work to *Current Law Index* though the extent of its coverage is less. It has recently expanded its coverage of Commonwealth journals. It commenced publication in 1908.

### vii. INDEX TO PERIODICAL ARTICLES RELATED TO LAW (UNITED STATES)

This covers many of the journals not covered in the two previous sources. It commenced publication in 1958.

### viii. INDEX TO FOREIGN LEGAL PERIODICALS (UNITED STATES)

This index is different in scope from the others being confined to international law, comparative law and legal systems other than common law. It commenced publication in 1960.

### ix. HALSBURY'S LAWS

This lists selected articles by subject in the *Monthly Review*. The list is tabulated in the tables section of the *Current Service*.

## Abbreviations

Journal articles are normally cited by an abbreviated version of the journal title. Many journal abbreviations are also listed in the works which give report abbreviations. (See 3.1)

# WORKS MENTIONED

Raistrick, Donald
***Lawyers Law Books: a practical index to legal literature. 2nd ed.***
(Professional Books Reference Library No1)
Abingdon, Professional Books, 1985

Hammick's Law Bookshop
***Law Book Catalogue***
Annual

***Legal Journals Index***
Hebden Bridge, Legal Information Resources, 1986-

***Current Law Index***
Belmont, California, Information Access Co, 1980-

***Index to Legal Periodicals***
New York, HW Wilson, 1908-

***Index to Periodical Articles Related to Law***
Dobbs Ferry, New York, Oceana, 1958-

***Index to Foreign Legal Periodicals***
Chicago, Illinois, AALL, 1960-

# Chapter 3: LAW REPORTS

The overwhelming majority of legal decisions in England and Wales are never reported at all. Superior courts may deal with well in excess of 20,000 cases a year, of which as few as 420 are likely to be reported in a general series like *All England Law Reports*. The following are the criteria by which a case may be selected for inclusion in *All E R*:

- it makes new law by dealing with a novel situation, or by extending the application of existing principles;
- it clarifies conflicting decisions of lower courts;
- it interprets legislation likely to have a wide application;
- it interprets a clause commonly found in legal documents;
- it clarifies an important point of practice or procedure.

On the basis of these very precise criteria one would expect most decisions to fall outside the net of reportability, and so they do. Nevertheless, you will often see footnotes in texts referring you to a case which remains unreported. There is always a chance that a report might have been published after the date of completion of your text, so it is still worth checking some of the sources described below.

## 3.1 Abbreviations

You will quickly begin to recognise the abbreviations for the more generally used series of reports. From time to time, you will come across abbreviations you have never seen before when it will be necessary to consult one of a number of works which expand abbreviations. This is a selection of the more readily available works:

- *Index to Legal Citations and Abbreviations*
- *The Digest*
- *Halsbury's Laws of England*
- *Osborn's Concise Law Dictionary*
- *Effective Legal Research* (For US abbreviations)
- *Current Law*

## 3.2 Early cases

Reports of the earliest cases can be found in the *Year Books* which extend from about 1260 to 1535. They are written in Law French and are as much social and historical as legal documents. These texts have been variously re-edited and published but being of largely academic interest, it is very unusual for there to be much need to consult them in ordinary practice.

In 1536 individual lawyers started to produce reports of cases. These reports, some series lasting only a year or two and of widely differing quality, are known by the names of their individual reporters or collectively as "nominate" reports. Such reporting lasted until 1865. Only the largest long established law libraries have holdings of the nominate reports as originally published.

Many of these nominate reports and some older cases have been reprinted in the *English Reports*, covering the years 1220 to 1865. There is an alphabetical table of cases in the last two volumes which you need if you do not have the *English Reports* reference.

Another collection is the *Revised Reports* covering the years 1786 to 1866, being reports of cases in the superior courts of common law and equity which were considered to be of value to the profession at the time the collection was published (1891 to 1920).

A third collection is the *All England Law Reports Reprint* covering headnotes and annotations from selected "authorised" reports from the years 1558 to 1842 and selected Law Times Reports from 1943-1935 . Additional cases, many of them from the Law Reports from the period 1861 to 1935 were published in "extension" volumes for the benefit of Australian lawyers.

## 3.3 Modern cases

### 3.3.1 General cases

In 1865 the Bar took steps to improve the anarchic state of law reporting by setting up its own reporting system run by the Incorporated Council of Law Reporting. The resulting series is called simply *The Law Reports*. Judges revise the reports before publication and they are semi-official to the extent that it is a Law Reports version which should be cited in court whenever possible. These reports are generally the most lengthy and include the arguments of counsel. But it should be remembered that they rarely appear less than six months from the date of the decision. As the structure of the court system has changed over the years, so the number of the titles of the sets in this series have varied. This means that the citations have also changed. Currently there are four series:

- Appeal Cases covering House of Lords and Privy Council decisions
- Chancery Division
- Family Division
- Queens Bench Division covering admiralty, commercial and Court of Appeal civil and criminal decisions.

Because of the delay in the publication of cases in *The Law Reports*, a new service was introduced in 1953 entitled *Weekly Law Reports*. These reports do not include the arguments of counsel and are not revised, but have a publication cycle of six weeks to five months from the date of the decision and some very important decisions appear even more quickly. Cases are reported in three volumes, those in the second and third volumes appear subsequently in *The Law Reports*, those in the first do not.

The series most popular with practitioners is the *All England Law Reports* which has been published by Butterworths since 1936. These reports do not contain the arguments of counsel and are not revised by judges. They do contain cross references to other works such as *The Digest* and *Halsbury's Laws of England*, but cases tend not to be reported as quickly as in the *Weekly Law Reports*.

From time to time you may well encounter citations to reports which have ceased publication such as *Law Journal Reports*, *Law Times Reports* and *Weekly Notes*, as well as reports from other common law jurisdictions. In general, these sets are likely to be found in only the larger law libraries. Frequently abstracts of such reports will appear in *The Digest* and these may supply sufficient information.

It should be noted that by a Practice Direction of 6th December 1991 ([1991] 1 W.L.R. 1) Lord Donaldson ruled that in the Court of Appeal as in the House of Lords the general rule is that reports published by the Incorporated Council of Law Reporting should be cited in preference to other series where there is a choice. The reason for this is that the other series will not necessarily contain the arguments of counsel and may be less readily available to the court.

### 3.3.2 Case notes

Many legal journals publish notes of decisions, of which the *Law Society's Gazette*, the *New Law Journal* and the *Solicitor's Journal* are among the more frequently cited. The following newspapers also publish reports of varying length and quality: *Financial Times*, *Guardian*, *Independent*, *Times* and *Lloyd's List*. It is more than possible that the same decision will be noted in all of these sources, and equally true that one particular decision may appear in only one of them. There are no hard and fast rules about this, though you can expect to see a fuller report of a significant decision eventually appearing in one or more of the general series mentioned above.

The importance of the case notes in these series is not so much their lasting value as that decisions can be read soon after they were made. Newspaper reports sometimes appear on the following day and certainly within a few weeks.

### 3.3.3 Specialist reports

Many areas of law have specialist series of reports, as well as the case notes appearing in specialist journals. This is the inevitable consequence of increasing specialisation in legal practice, with new sources appearing all the time. You will soon become familiar with the specialist sources in the areas of law in which you find yourself working. Appendix 2 lists selected reports.

## 3.4 Electronic sources

LEXIS includes the overwhelming majority of published law reports, including *The Law Reports* from 1945 to date. Moreover, there are approximately 3,000 unreported cases from the Court of Appeal Civil Division recorded from transcripts. You will also find full transcripts of judgments where the only published report is from the *Times* newspaper. When using LEXIS it is important to remember that a search strategy confined

to catchwords or headnotes will automatically exclude transcripts.

JUSTIS contains the *Weekly Law Reports*, as well as some Scots law reports.

## 3.5 Legal Research Using Law Reports

### 3.5.1 Tracing law reports where only the names of the parties are known

From time to time you will be asked to find a report of a case where only the names of the parties are known, or you might need an alternative reference if the cited report is unavailable. Perhaps you need a longer or more reliable report than the one you have to hand. The sources which follow are amongst those which are likely to help. With experience you will learn which is the most appropriate source to search first, depending on your specific needs at the time.

#### i. CURRENT LAW CASE CITATOR

The volumes of the Case Citator (currently three) and the most recent monthly issue of *Current Law* should give you a list of reported cases from 1947 to date together with references to those earlier cases which have been judicially noticed since 1947. With a much reported case, you will see the preferred order in which reports should be cited. Occasionally you will find references to unreported cases.

#### ii. THE DIGEST

This work summarises many of the reported English cases, together with some from other common law jurisdictions. There is a *Consolidated Table of Cases* to 1991, brought up to date by a table of cases to be found in the *Annual Cumulative Supplement*. The table of cases refers you only to the appropriate subject volume. Then you have to consult the volume index to find the page or paragraph number for the case in question.

*The Digest* is accompanied by a handy pamphlet which explains in detail how the work should be used.

#### iii. LAW REPORTS INDEXES

The tables of cases in the *Law Reports* and the *All England Law Reports* might help. The *Law Reports Indexes* cover the period 1951 to date in decennial indexes. The current 10 year period is covered by the *Cumulative Index 1981-1990*, the "Red Index" for 1991 plus the "Pink Index" which appears periodically. The Index has an eclectic coverage, but it does cover all the major English report series and some specialist series. The Pink Index can be updated by the index in the *Weekly Law Reports* parts.

The *All England Law Reports Consolidated Tables and Index* covers the period 1936-1989 with indexes for the current year appearing at irregular intervals throughout the year. There is a Cumulative Tables and Index for 1990-91.

Most legal textbooks have a table of cases discussed at the beginning of the work so if you are sure of the subject area you are researching this may be a useful source.

### iv. HALSBURY'S LAWS OF ENGLAND

There is a two volume table of cases published as part of *Halsbury's Laws of England*. If you happen to know the year of the case, the *Annual Abridgement* to *Halsbury's Laws* might be a convenient short cut.

### v. LEGAL JOURNALS INDEX

For recent cases, particularly in specialised areas of law such as building and construction, this index will identify reports in journals, often providing references to the general series of reports as well. Remember that some cases may only ever be reported in journals. Journal reports also appear quickly.

### vi. DAILY LAW REPORTS INDEX

This work commenced publication in 1988 and gives detailed references to newspaper law reports. Approximately 1,000 individual cases are reported in daily newspapers each year. You can search by subject and by legislation in exactly the same way as with *Legal Journals Index*. It is also possible to search by the names of either party. This index is published fortnightly, cumulating quarterly and annually. The cumulation volumes give citations to the general series of reports. It is inevitable that some cases will only ever be reported in newspapers. However, if all you have is a newspaper law report be sure to check whether a better report has been subsequently published. A report from one of the general series will always be preferred to a newspaper law report.

### vii. LAWTEL

There is a table of cases from 1980 to date which covers the main series of reports as well as some of the newspapers.

### viii. LEXIS

For cases decided after 1945 it is possible to use LEXIS simply to identify a report, though this is probably an expensive solution, as it will cost as much as a complex subject search. The importance of LEXIS in identifying cases is that it holds the unreported cases in the Court of Appeal Civil Division, as well as all the main published series of law reports, though not necessarily those appearing in journals. You cannot assume that because you have searched LEXIS it is unnecessary to check other sources as well. LEXIS may give you a transcipt and lead you to suppose that the decision is unreported whereas it may have been covered by a set of reports beyond the scope of LEXIS. Also, remember that the transcript of an otherwise unreported case in LEXIS may be extremely lengthy. It has been known to take longer than an hour to print a case from LEXIS.

ix. **ENGLISH REPORTS INDEX**

Volumes 177 and 178 contain an Index to all the cases reported in the *English Reports*.

The *English Reports* also contain a *Chart of Reports* which will enable you to interpret unfathomable abbreviations such as "3 Russ." This is arranged alphabetically by the name of the reporter and tells you the number of volumes in each series and which volume of the *English Reports* they appear in. It also gives the abbreviation for each series and the approximate period covered. This can be very useful when you have an incomplete reference or are not quite sure of the exact series.

### 3.5.2 Tracing the status of a case

When the report of a case has been read, and found to be on point, the next question usually concerns whether or not it is still good law. A number of expressions might be used when an earlier case is judicially noticed in a later judgment. The following are used most commonly in works of legal reference: affirmed, applied, approved, considered, disapproved, distinguished, doubted, explained, extended, followed, not followed, overruled, referred to, and reversed. Check that you understand what is meant by these expressions when you come across them. Farrar's *Introduction to Legal Method* contains a useful discussion of case law which considers these terms. Another explanation of their meanings can be found in *The Digest* volumes (3.4.3).

In the United Kingdom there is no central system for recording those cases which have been judicially noticed. American lawyers are much better served in this and in a number of other respects. However, here are some of the sources you can use when attempting to establish the status of a case.

i. **CURRENT LAW CASE CITATOR**

The Case Citator annotates reported cases which have been judicially noticed, with references to the appropriate volumes of the *Current Law Yearbook* where the case is digested. The annotating cases will all be in the period 1947 to date.

ii. **THE DIGEST**

The digest of each case is followed by the relevant citations which indicate how that case has been annotated in later cases. Remember that a given case may be digested under more than one subject heading, and that it is also necessary to use the *Continuation Volumes* and *Cumulative Supplement* as well as the appropriate subject volume(s). You might feel more confident if you ask someone to explain the intricacies of *The Digest* before you attempt to make serious use of it. (See further Section 3.5.3ii and the problem on the writ ne exeat regno in the case problems section). It is most helpful for tracing old cases but is probably not worth using for tracing very recent cases.

iii. **LEXIS**

You will always find many more recent annotated cases with a LEXIS search than by any other means, not the least because of the inclusion of unreported cases in the Court of Appeal Civil Division. The LEXIS command protocol makes it possible to search according to whether the annotated case is mentioned in the judgment or cited by counsel but it probably makes more sense to do a general search just using some component of the names of the parties in the case. Remember always, but particularly in this context, that the citation of cases in reports is frequently lackadaisical if not entirely whimsical, and that judges are rarely any more precise in the way that they cite cases than anyone else. You must take this into account when you are devising a strategy which will retrieve references to cases by name. Remember also that LEXIS is less useful for older cases than the *The Digest*.

iv. **LAW REPORTS INDEXES**

These also tell you when a case has been judicially considered.

### 3.5.3 Finding cases by subject

Tracing cases by subject is one of the more difficult processes in legal research. A successful search will probably have involved the consultation of a wide range of sources and where you choose to start with a given research problem will be a matter of experience in using the various tools at your disposal, as well as your knowledge of the substantive point of law in question.

If there is a golden rule it is that you should make use of all the sources available to you. You would be very ill-advised to suppose that any single source, whatever its claims, will give you access to all you need to know. Each and every tool that you use is likely to be found wanting in some respect but used in conjunction they are likely to yield impressive results. In any event, you are bound to spot inaccuracies and oddities after you have been using these services for any length of time. Do not be surprised by this, and be warned that errors and inconsistencies do exist.

i. **BOOKS**

Try using books first. At the very least you should get some strong pointers as to the nature of the ground over which you must travel. Even if you do not have access to a book specifically on the matter in hand, you are well advised to look at *Halsbury's Laws of England* which is remarkably well foot-noted with references to case law. In litigation matters, the *Supreme Court Practice*, or "White Book" as it is generally known, is a mine of references to case law on questions of procedure.

ii. **THE DIGEST**

This is the ultimate encyclopaedic guide to case law and you have a right to be disappointed if you fail to discover a leading case from this source, particularly if it dates from some time in the past. You are likely to be less successful if you seek recent case law. *The Digest* contains abstracts of cases with citations to fuller reports. The abstracts are arranged by broad subject topics which are then divided into more specific subject areas. It aims to include most English cases plus some Scottish, Irish and Commonwealth cases. The current edition is known as the *Green Band Edition* as the volumes have a green band on their spine. Publication of these volumes is now complete and you will notice that some of them have *Second Reissue* on their spines. This is because the series is in a constant state of revision and individual volumes are brought up to date and reissued from time to time.

You will need to use the *Consolidated Index*, which has now been published in three volumes: A-D, E-O, P-Z (1992) and is much more detailed than the 1990 one volume *Consolidated Index*. Some of the earlier subject volumes have detailed indexes, but you will not find them in the later reissued volumes. If you are reasonably confident as to your subject matter, the table of contents for each title may help you to reach the specific subject of your search. As well as the appropriate subject volume, you must consult the *Cumulative Supplement* and the *Continuation Volumes* to ensure that you are as up to date as the work permits.

The following explanation is intended to give you some guidance on how to use *The Digest.* If you were asked to find some information about bills of exchange, begin with the *Consolidated Index* A-D 1992. The references are as follows:-

**BILL OF EXCHANGE**
acceptance of, as payment **26** *Guar* 1449

This refers you to Volume 26 which covers guarantees and to paragraph 1449

This reference will not work if a subsequent reissue volume has appeared. For example, if you are researching drawing up an injunction, the *Consolidated Index* E-O 1992 reference is to :-

**INJUNCTION**
order, the
drawing up **28(2)** *Injun* 1288

Unfortunately, Volume 28(2) has been replaced by a Second Reissue volume and Vol. 28(2) now covers Income and Corporation Tax. You therefore need to look at Volume 28(4) Second Reissue which covers injunctions. At the back of this volume there is an English case adaptor which gives you the old paragraph number next to the new paragraph number. Thus, paragraph 1288 is now paragraph 6830 in the Second Reissue.

*Continuation Volumes*

You will then need to update your research by checking the *Continuation Volumes* D,E,F,G & H. 1986-90. These include new cases heard over the past few years (D 1971-1975; E 1976-1979; F 1980-1983; G 1984-1985; H 1986-1990). They are arranged to key in with the main subject volumes.

*Cumulative Supplement*

This will bring your research up to date. It extends the *Consolidated Table of Cases* (1991) to the present and it indicates where further changes and cases have been added to the green band volumes. It also is keyed into the subject arrangement of the Green Band volumes. Cases in the *Cumulative Supplement* appear in the Index followed by the reference CVD, CVE, CVF etc.

If you are trying to update research on a particular case, check the *Consolidated Table of Cases* if it is a pre-1991 case and the *Cumulative Supplement* if it is a post 1991 case. This will lead you to the relevant subject area and will digest any further cases.

### iii. LEGAL JOURNALS INDEX

There are two respects in which this source helps with recent cases. In the first place, you can search on very precise subject terms, and also subject terms in combination. This will yield both legal journal reports as well as articles dealing with particular cases. Secondly, you can use references to articles on a specific subject to trace relevant case law. An article in a legal journal which discusses a subject of law can scarcely avoid mentioning the leading cases in that area. This is a surprisingly effective method of finding a leading case.

### iv. LAWTEL

LAWTEL will reveal legal sources by a subject search. In addition to digesting cases by subject for the period 1980 to date, it will sometimes provide references to older case law when this has been the subject of a LAWTEL Research Bureau enquiry. It also has a valuable section on personal injury awards which complements the standard sources on quantum of damages.

### v. LEXIS

Provided that you can transcribe the research problem into the words which would be used by judges when discussing relevant cases, LEXIS is a vital weapon in the armoury of legal research. However, the results will be no better than the search strategy used. Salesmen will tell you that it is your legal knowledge which prevents you from making inexpert use of LEXIS. Do not be misled into a false sense of security by this appeal to your vanity. It is essential to have thought through the research problem with considerable clarity, and to have devised a strategy which has some promise of delivering the goods, before you switch on the machine. Lateral thinking will help here. Making effective use of LEXIS is more than pressing keys on a keyboard. Pressing keys is the easy part. Perhaps the greatest danger of all lies in supposing that you have made good use of LEXIS when you have not. Even though you may have discovered some relevant material, there might have been much more which your strategy failed to retrieve. And, if you are offered LEXIS training do not regard it as a period of relaxation.

### vi. DAILY LAW REPORTS INDEX

As has been noted above, this work abstracts and indexes the law reports appearing in daily newspapers. The index consists of a detailed abstract of each case together with a keyword index, and an index to the legislation considered. In each quarterly cumulation there is a list of citations to full reports in the major series. The index cumulates quarterly and annually and can be searched electronically.

### vii. CURRENT LAW

This is published monthly and digests new reported cases (as well as legislation and other legal developments) by subject. Each of the monthly issues contains a cumulative index for the year to date. The monthly issues cumulate into the *Yearbook*, which itself has cumulative indexes in the so-called "master volumes". It is worth spending some time finding out what you can do with *Current Law*. There are few circumstances where it yields no information at all.

### viii. HALSBURYS LAWS

This can prove to be a surprisingly useful source for tracing recent cases by subject as the *Monthly Reviews* contain abstracts of recent cases which are keyed into the main subject volumes.

### ix. LAW REPORTS INDEXES

These contain indexes by subject matter.

### x. NEWSPAPER DATABASES

It is easy to forget how often an interesting legal development is reported in the press, though it may not merit a newspaper law report. Quantum of damage for personal injury is a good example. There are a number of online services such as Profile and Textline which offer access to newspapers in full text, and which may be a useful means of access to case law if the circumstances warrant it.

### 3.5.4 Finding cases interpreting legislation

You may be asked to find out whether a particular Act or section of an Act has been judicially considered. If so a similar range of sources as are used for making a subject search of case law can be used, although in slightly different ways.

i. **Books**

As law books generally have tables of cases, so they usually have tables of statutes and these may help you discover which decisions concern a particular piece of legislation. Some of the large subject encyclopaedias are particularly useful in this respect, often taking you directly to the level of a sub-section.

ii. **Halsbury's Statutes**

Cases are noted in the annotations. Later cases are noted in the *Cumulative Supplement* and the *Noter-up.*

iii. **Current Law Legislation Citator**

As well as the case citator, there is a legislation citator which gives details of cases decided under particular acts and sections covering the post-1947 years. This is kept up to date by the service volume of *Current Law Statutes Annotated.* This should lead you to some of the more important cases decided under the legislation in question.

iv. **Law Reports Indexes**

The *Law Reports Index* and the *All England Law Reports Index* include tables of statutes which have been judicially considered.

v. **Legal Journals Index**

The legislation index will assist in tracing cases reported in legal journals under particular sections of statutes, statutory instruments, Rules of the Supreme Court etc.

vi. **Daily Law Reports Index**

This work indexes newspaper law reports according to legislative instrument in a similar way to *Legal Journals Index.*

vii. **Lawtel**

LAWTEL has a statute citator which records cases reported after 1980 by statute subdivided by section.

viii. **LEXIS**

LEXIS can be used for this type of search but remember that it is difficult to devise a search strategy which can be relied upon to achieve the desired result. For example, a judge is likely to refer to "section 49 of the 1977 Act" having named the Act in full a few sentences back. Thus, a search on section 49 within say 15 words of the name of an Act cited in full, may fail to retrieve a relevant case. For the same reason you are advised not to attempt to search on sub-sections at all. On the other hand, if you make your search too general, you are likely to be plagued with irrelevant references.

### 3.5.5 Finding cases interpreting statutory instruments

The main sources to use when establishing whether an SI has been judicially considered are indexes to the general series of law reports; *Current Law* and the *Current Law Yearbook*. It is also possible to search the cases file in the ENGGEN (English General Library) on LEXIS under the title of an instrument but considerable care needs to be exercised in devising an appropriate search strategy.

# WORKS MENTIONED

Raistrick, Donald
***Index to legal citations and abbreviations***
Abingdon, Professional Books, 1981

Price, M.O.
***Effective legal research*** . 4th ed.
Boston, Little Brown, 1979

***Current Law***
London, Sweet & Maxwell, 1947-
Monthly

Osborn
***Concise Law Dictionary***. 7th ed.
London, Sweet & Maxwell, 1983

***English Reports***
1220-1865
London, Stevens
178 vols.

***Revised Reports***
1786-1866
London, Stevens
152 vols.

***All England Law Reports Reprint***
1558-1935
London, Butterworths
36 vols.
Extension vols 1861-1935
London, Butterworths
16 vols.

***Law Reports***
1865-
London, Incorporated Council of Law Reporting
Digest and Index 1865-1950
12 vols.
Consolidated Index 1951-1990
4 vols.
Consolidated Index 1991
Cumulative Index 1992
Three times a year and annual

*Weekly Law Reports*
1953-
London, Incorporated Council of Law Reporting

*Law Journal Reports*
1822-1831
London, Law Journal
9 vols.
1832-1949
118 vols.

*Law Times Reports*
1843-1965
London, Butterworths
236 vols.

*Weekly Notes*
1866-1952
London, Incorporated Council of Law Reporting
87 vols.

Farrar, J.
***Introduction to legal method***. 3rd ed.
London, Sweet & Maxwell, 1990

## Legal Research Using Law Reports

### Practical Examples

It is recommended that you work through these problems using the books listed as this should give you a clearer idea of the steps involved in researching the problems. Merely reading through these examples will only serve to confuse!

The problems are keyed in to the relevant paragraph numbers in the text.

## 3.5.1. Tracing law reports where only the names of the parties are known.

Two problems are illustrated for this exercise

A) **Find the case of** **Barber v Guardian Royal Exchange Assurance Group**

This example illustrates research into recent cases

## CHECK

1) **CURRENT LAW CASE CITATOR**

**Current Law Case Citator 1947-1976**

No entry

**Current Law Case Citator 1977-1988**

Barber v Guardian Royal Exchange Assurance Group; Roberts v Tate & Lyle Food and Distribution [1983] I.C.R. 521; [1983] I.R.L.R. 240; [1986] E.C.R. 703; E.A.T. *Digested* 83/**1294**
*Considered* 86/1191
*Approved* 88/1325

The figures appearing in bold type indicate that the case is digested in the 1983 yearbook at paragraph 1294. This appears under a series of catchwords followed by an abstract of the case:

**1294 Sex discrimination - retirement - different benefits**

[Sex Discrimination Act 1975 **(c.65) s.6(4)**.]

The test of whether a complaint alleging sex discrimination is outside the ambit of the statute because it relates to retirement........

and then a reference to it thus:-

ROBERTS v TATE & LYLE FOOD AND DISTRIBUTION; BARBER v GUARDIAN ROYAL EXCHANGE ASSURANCE GROUP [1983] I.C.R. 521, E.A.T.

**NOTE:** That Roberts v Tate & Lyle Food and Distribution and Barber v Guardian Royal Exchange Assurance Group were heard together in the Employment Appeal Tribunal because they covered such similar subject matter and that Roberts appears first. By the time they reach the European Court, Roberts has disappeared. This practice can cause problems with citations. Note also that the European Court Reports (E.C.R.) reference is to the European Court hearing in the Roberts Case (Case 151/84). This is confusing as the other references are not to the European Court decision.

The "Considered" reference relates to an entry in the 1986 Yearbook at paragraph 1191 for Hayward v Cammell Laird Shipbuilders [1986] I.R.L.R., 287 EAT, where the EAT considered the tribunal's judgment in Barber.

Similarly, the "Approved" reference relates to a case digested at paragraph 1325 of the 1988 Yearbook. In this case, Duke v G.E.C. Reliance (Formerly Reliance Systems) [1988] 2 W.L.R. 359, HL, the House of Lords approved the EAT decision in Barber

**Current Law Case Citator 1989/91**

Barber v Guardian Royal Exchange Assurance Group (No. C-262/88) [1991] Q.B. 344; [1991] 2 W.L.R. 72; [1990] 2 All E.R. 660; [1990] I.C.R. 616; [1990] I.R.L.R. 240; [1990] E.C.R. 1-1889; [1990] 2 C.M.L.R. 513; (1990) New L.J. 925, European Ct ....... *Digested* 90/**1915**
*Applied* 91/1636, 1669

Paragraph 1915 of the 1990 Yearbook has the following entry:-

**1915 Redundancy - age limit for eligibility for pension or redundancy - different age qualifications for men and women - whether contrary to principle of equal pay - whether pension "pay"**

Pensions paid to an employee under a contracted-out private pension-scheme fall within the meaning of pay in Art.119 of the EEC Treaty............

BARBER v GUARDIAN ROYAL EXCHANGE ASSURANCE GROUP (No. 262/88) [1990] 2 All E.R. 660, European Ct.

This entry relates to a referral by the Court of Appeal to the European Court of Justice for its opinion on questions arising out of the appeal from the Employment Appeal Tribunal. There is no report of the Court of Appeal hearing.

The "Applied" references relate to cases digested at paragraphs 1636 and 1669 of the 1991 Yearbook. In these cases, McKechnie v UBM Building Supplies (Southern) [1991] I.R.L.R. 283, EAT and Roberts v Birds Eye Wall's [1990] I.C.R. 43, EAT, the Employment Appeal Tribunal applied the EAT decision in Barber.

**Current Law Monthly Digest Parts**

The Cumulative Table of Cases contained in each monthly digest has a list of recent cases. The June issue, [1992] 6 C.L., has the following entry:-

BARBER v GUARDIAN ROYAL EXCHANGE ASSURANCE GROUP, Jan 221

The reference at paragraph 221 of the January 1992 issue relates to the case Roscoe v Hick Hargreaves & Co [1991] I.C.R. 501, Industrial Tribunal, where Barber was applied.

## 2) THE DIGEST

**Consolidated Table of Cases 1991 A-C**

No entry!

**Cumulative Supplement 1992**

There is a Table of Cases near the beginning of the volume

BARBER v GUARDIAN ROYAL EXCHANGE ASSURANCE GROUP (1990) 20 Empt 4509a (ii), 37(1) Pensions 50

Turn to section 20, Employment, in the Cumulative Supplement and follow the numbered paragraphs through to 4509 and under 4509a (ii) there is a digest of Barber v Guardian Royal Exchange Assurance Group and at the end a reference

BARBER v GUARDIAN ROYAL EXCHANGE ASSURANCE GROUP [1990] 2 All E.R. 660, (1990) Times, 18 May, ECJ

## 3) LAW REPORTS INDEXES

**(i) Law Reports Index**

This index covers the years 1951 to date in decennial volumes. Where the date of the case is not known, this is not the best index to check. The most recent issues of this index cover 1981-1990 ("Red Index") then 1991 ("Red Index") and then 1992 ("Pink Index").

**Red Index 1981-1990**

Barber v Guardian Royal Exchange Assurance Group (Case C262/88) [1991] 2 W.L.R. 72; [1990] I.C.R. 616; [1990] 2 All E.R. 660, ECJ.

Barber v Guardian Royal Exchange Assurance Group (*See*) Roberts v Tate & Lyle Food and Distribution Ltd

The entry under Roberts refers to the EAT decision:-

Roberts v Tate & Lyle Food and Distribution Ltd [1983] I.C.R. 521, EAT

**Red Index 1991**

Barber v Guardian Royal Exchange Assurance Group (Case C262/88) [1991] 1 Q.B. 344; [1991] 2 W.L.R. 72; [1990] 2 All E.R. 660; [1990] I.C.R. 616, ECJ

**Pink Index 1992**

No entry

(ii) **All England Law Reports Index**

**Consolidated Tables and Index 1936-1989**

Vol. 1: Tables includes those cases judicially considered within the main case name index

It does not list Barber v Guardian Royal Exchange Assurance Group

This is because this index only gives references to All England Law Reports between 1936-1989

**Cumulative Tables and Index 1990-91**

The cases reported and considered list contains the following entry:

Barber v Guardian Royal Exchange Assurance Group (Case C-262/88) [1990] **2** 660, CJEC

This, of course, refers to Volume 2 of the 1990 All England Reports at page 660, and note that this index refers to the ECJ as the CJEC (Court of Justice of the European Communities).

**Current Tables and Index 1992 - Issue 2**

No entry

4) **HALSBURY'S LAWS**

**Consolidated Table of Cases**
Vol. 54 (1992)

No entry

**Cumulative Supplement 1992**

See Table of Cases near the beginning of Part 1

Barber v Guardian Royal Exchange Assurance Group C262/88 [1991] 1 QB 344, [1990] 2 All E.R. 660, [1990] 2 WLR 72, [1990] 2 CMLR 513, ECJ
1990 Abr 2906 ..... **52** 21:12,21:14

**Current Service**

Table of Cases Referred to in Monthly Reviews

No entry

**B) Find the case of <u>Dearle v Hall</u>. Has it been considered recently?**

This example has been included as it illustrates research using older cases.

## CHECK

### 1) CURRENT LAW CASE CITATOR

**Current Law Case Citator 1947-1976**

Dearle v Hall (1828) 3 Russ. 1 *Distinguished* 58/3089

Having found the reference, it must be interpreted.
The best way of doing this is to check an abbreviations list (see **3.1**).
An alternative approach, which may produce the answer more quickly and also supply an abstract of the case, is a check in the Case Index to the *Digest* as this comprehensively covers older cases.

**Current Law Case Citator 1977-88**

Dearle v Hall (1828) 3 Russ. 1 ...................... *Applied* 88/2060
*Referred* to 88/3175

**Current Law Case Citator 1989/91**

Dearle v Hall (1828) 3 Russ. 1 ...................... *Considered* 89/2162

To see the case considering Dearle v Hall check the entry in the 1989 Yearbook at paragraph 2162. This leads you to the case of <u>Galinski v McHugh</u> on notice under s.4 Landlord and Tenant Act 1954 but there is no mention of consideration of <u>Dearle v Hall</u>. A check through nearby entries reveals that <u>Dearle v Hall</u> was considered in in the case cited at entry 2164 on whether a notice was valid against a receiver.

**NOTE:** Not only is the main paragraph reference incorrect, but the reference is also incorrect as it gives 3 **Rass** and not **Russ.**

**Current Law Monthly Digest June [1992] 6 C.L.**

No entry

### 2) THE DIGEST

**Consolidated Table of Cases 1991 D-I**

No entry under "Dearle" or "Hall".

It seems that the case is not covered in the Digest. However, if you have followed up any of the references above, you will know that the case concerns choses in action. This subject is covered in volume 8(2) of the Digest. It is therefore necessary to check in the *Table of Cases* at the beginning of Vol.8(2) to locate the case where it does not appear! The only way of locating it is to scan through the contents pages of this volume where a little diligent research will locate it under

**NOTICE OF ASSIGNMENT**
**(9) Priority**
(i) BY NOTICE
*1. As between assignees*
**A The Rule in Dearle v Hall** ..... 93

This gives an abstract of the case and some alternative references:

[1824-34] All E.R. Rep. 28; 3 Russ. 1; 38 E.R. 475, L.C.

The All E.R. Rep. is a reference to the *All England Law Reports Reprint* (see **3.2**). The E.R. reference is to the *English Reports* (see **3.2**) and the Russ. reference is to *Russell's Reports*, one of the series of Nominate Reports (see **3.2**). (The abbreviation L.C. means that the case was heard in the Chancery Division before the Lord Chancellor). Your library is unlikely to have the Nominate Reports. If it has the *English Reports*, this is the best series to check.

**NOTE:** This is not very helpful unless you happen to know that Dearle v Hall is about notice of assignment of choses in action.

3) **ENGLISH REPORTS**

**Index of Cases Vols 177-178**

Dearle v Hall, 3 Russ. 1, 48 ..... **38** 475,492

The case appears in Volume 38. There are two page references, the second one being to the appeal.

The abbreviation Russ. is for *Russell's Reports* which cover the period 1823-1829 in the Chancery Division and as discovered above, they are reprinted in Vol. 38.

You will note that the pages in the *English Reports* also give details of the Nominate Report reference at the top left and right margins on each page.

4) **LEGAL JOURNALS INDEX**

To ascertain whether there has been any up-to-date commentary on this case, it is worth checking here. A database search reveals three recent articles

**ASSIGNMENT. Book debts. Corporate insolvency. Passing of property. Priorities**
Retention of title - rule in Dearle v Hall. (Dispute between unpaid seller and factoring company in whose favour insolvent buyer had executed assignment of book debts). By L.S. Sealy.
*C.L.J. 1992, 51(1), 19-21*

**ASSIGNMENT. Book debts. Notice. Priorities**
Priorities: equitable versus legal assignments of book debts. (Whether rule in Dearle v Hall governs such priorities). By Fidelis Oditah.
*O.J.L.S. 1989, 9(4), 513-533*

**ASSIGNMENT. Debts. Floating charges. Notice. Priorities**
Priority of assignments - a review of the application of the rule in Dearle v Hall to floating charges. (Priority given to first assignee of debt to notify debtor).
*C. & F.L. 1988, 1(3), 18-20*

## 3.5.2 Tracing the status of a case

**Is the 1986 report of AG Securities v Vaughan still good law? Has it been disapproved?**

Because we know that this is a recent case, there is unlikely to be very much judicial comment and it will only be necessary to check the more up to date sources.

## CHECK

1) **CURRENT LAW CASE CITATOR**

**Current Law Case Citator 1977-1988**

A.G. Securities v Vaughan; Antoniades v Villiers [1988] 3 W.L.R. 1205; (1988) 132 S.J. 1638; [1988] 3 All E.R. 1058; [1988] 47 E.G. 193; (1988) 138 N.L.J. 325; [1989] L.S.Gaz. January 5, 39, HL; reversing [1988] 2 W.L.R. 689 ......................Digested 88/**2026**

This refers to the entry in the 1988 Yearbook at paragraph 2026 which appears under a series of catchwords followed by an abstract of the case:

**2026 Exclusive occupation - more than one occupier - statutory protection.** Where the landlord makes a pretence at conferring on himself power to introduce new occupiers, which it is never intended to use.....

and then a reference to it thus:-

A.G. SECURITIES v VAUGHAN; ANTONIADES v VILLIERS, *The Times*, November 11, 1988 HL

**NOTE**: That AG Securities v Vaughan and Antoniades v Villiers were heard together in the House of Lords because they covered such similar subject matter. This practice is increasing and can cause problems with citations.

**Current Law Case Citator 1989/91**

*Digested* 89/**2143**
*Applied* 89/2145, 2146
*Considered* 89/2144, 2145

This gives a reference in bold to the paragraph where the case is digested plus four references to paragraph numbers of recent cases in the 1989 Yearbook in which the case was judicially considered.

**Current Law Monthly Parts**

Cumulative Table of Cases

January-June 1992

A.G. SECURITIES v VAUGHAN; ANTONIADES v VILLIERS, Feb 275; Mar 306

This refers to paragraph 306 in the March Monthly Digest and paragraph 275 in the February Monthly Digest:

Mar 306
KAY v MOSSBETTER, [1991] 39 E.G. 129, CA
(*A.G. Securities v Vaughan* considered)

Feb 275
NORRIS (T/A J. DAVIS & SON) v CHECKSFIELD [1991] I.C.R. 632, CA
(*A.G. Securities v Vaughan* distinguished)

## 2) THE DIGEST

**Consolidated Table of Cases 1991 A-C**

AG Securities v Vaughan and others (1988) **CVH**

**Continuation Volume H**

**Table of Cases**

AG Securities v Vaughan and others (1988): **31(1)** *L&T* 1703a(iii)

Turn to Vols 31(1) & (2) in Continuation Volume H and at paragraph 1703a(iii) there is a digest of the case plus a reference

AG SECURITIES v VAUGHAN AND OTHERS; ANTONIADES V VILLIERS AND ANOTHER [1988] 3 All E.R. 1058 (HL)

plus a note telling us that the decision of the Court of Appeal was reversed and a reference to the case of Stribling v Wickham (1989) Times, 27 March which applied this case

## 3) LAW REPORTS INDEXES

### i) Law Reports Index

**Red Index 1981-1990**

AG Securities v Vaughan [1990] 1 A.C. 417; [1988] 2 W.L.R. 689; [1988] 2 All E.R. 173, CA; [1990] 1 A.C. 417; [1988] 3 W.L.R. 1205; [1988] 3 All E.R. 1058 H.L.(E).

**NOTE:** The reference to H.L.(E) means that it is an English case.

**Red Index 1991**

No entry

**Pink Index 1992**

No entry

The *Law Reports Indexes* do not therefore contain as much information about this case as *Current Law Case Citator*.

ii) **All England Law Reports Index**

**Consolidated Tables and Index 1936-1989**

This index includes those cases judicially considered within the main case name index.
Vol. 1: Tables
This volume contains the following information:-

Cases reported and considered; Practice directions and notes; Statutes considered; Words and phrases considered

AG Securities v Vaughan [1988] **2** 173, CA
Reversed [1988] **3** 1058, HL

**Cumulative Tables and Index 1990-91**

No entry

**Current Tables and Index 1992 - Issue 2**

No entry

**NOTE:** This index only gives references to All England Law Reports. The Law Reports Indexes do not contain as much information about this case as Current Law Case Citator.

4) **HALSBURY'S LAWS**

**Consolidated Table of Cases**
**Vol. 54 (1992)**

No entry

**Cumulative Supplement 1992**

See Table of Cases near the beginning of the volume:

AG Securities v Vaughan [1990] 1 A.C. 417, [1988] 3 All E.R. 1058, [1988] 3 W.L.R. 1205, HL, 1988 Abr 1366 .............**27** 6,7

**NOTE:** These are the House of Lords decisions.

**Current Service**

Table of Cases Referred to in Monthly Reviews.

No entry

5) **LEGAL JOURNALS INDEX**

The case index can be used to find references to a case and comment on that case and a search of the database reveals 32 articles on this case.

6) **DAILY LAW REPORTS INDEX**

The fortnightly parts, quarterly cumulations and annual volumes contain case indexes, plus an index showing where cases are fully reported or the database can be searched to find the Court of Appeal and House of Lords decisions plus further reports which mention AG Securities v Vaughan.

7) **LAWTEL**

LAWTEL can be searched by case name. A search reveals notes of both the Court of Appeal and House of Lords decisions and shows that the former was overruled.

8) **LEXIS**

A LEXIS search will retrieve the main report, plus further reports which mention AG Securities v Vaughan. In this instance, twelve further reports were retrieved.

## 3.5.3 Finding cases by subject

**Are there any cases on marital rape?**

1) **BOOKS**

**Rayden and Jackson on Divorce**
This has a looseleaf service so is a good source to check for up-to-date information. The 16th edition has no index entry for rape or marital rape, but the entry under adultery refers you to the 15th edition.

Check the index to the 15th edition to find rape at p.227 in Chapter 7 of Part III where there is a review of case law, but note that Volume 1 is only up to date to 1988

**Noter-up in loose-leaf service**

No entries up to September 1991

**Butterworths Family Law Service**

**Rape**

Marital -
compellability, wife as witness, PACE 1984, **B5**
English law, **B5**
immunity, extinguishment, **B5**
Scottish law, **B5**

There is a review at B3 of cases including the up to date cases of R. v Crapper (1990) N.L.J.R. 1497, and R. v R [1991] 2 W.L.R. 1065, CA.

**NOTE:** Rayden is not as up to date as Butterworths. Note also the varied methods of citing New Law Journal Reports. The correct method is (1990) 140 N.L.J. Rep. 1497.

2) **THE DIGEST**

**Consolidated Index 1992**

There is nothing specific under CRIME DURING MARRIAGE

It is therefore necessary to check the contents pages of Vol. 27(1) Husband and Wife:-

**4 RIGHTS AND OBLIGATIONS OF PARTIES ARISING FROM MARRIAGE.**

**(3) Wrongs of husband and wife during marriage** 323

(i) CRIMES .... 323

There is nothing on rape at p.323

Crimes etc are included in paras 2813-2816

**Cumulative Supplement 1992**

Nothing appears under these paras.

### 3) CURRENT LAW

**Current Law Yearbook 1991**
Index



**975 Rape - buggery - husband and wife - whether marital exemption exists**

R. v C (RAPE: MARITAL EXEMPTION) [1991] 1 All E.R. 755, Simon Brown J.

**976 Rape - husband and wife - family protection order in existence - whether operates as withdrawal of consent to intercourse**

R. v SHAW [1991] Crim. L.R. 301, CA

**977 Rape - husband and wife - living apart - whether marital exemption exists**

R. v J (RAPE: MARITAL EXEMPTION) [1991] 1 All E.R. 759, Rougier J.

**978 Rape - husband and wife - whether marital exemption exists**

R. v R (RAPE: MARITAL EXEMPTION), *The Times*, October 24, 1991, HL

**1799 Marital Rape - standard of proof in matrimonial cases**

N v N, *The Times*, August 13, 1991 CA

**Current Law Monthly Parts June [1992] 6 C.L.**



Feb 127
**Rape - attempted rape - consent - whether marital exemption exists**

R. v R (RAPE: MARITAL EXEMPTION) [1991] 4 All E.R. 481, HL

## 4) HALSBURY'S LAWS

**Consolidated Index 1990 I-Z**

RAPE
husband and wife, **11(1)**, 515; **22**, 1117 n[1]

**Vol. 11(1)**

para 515 Husband and wife

A review of case law appears here but the most recent case is only 1988 - R. v Kowalski [1988] 1 F.L.R. 447

**Vol. 22**

para 1117 note 1 refers to three cases concerning the rape of a wife by her husband (none recent).

**Cumulative Supplement 1992 (Part 1)**

**Vol 11 (1) (reissue)**

**515 Husband and wife**
TEXT and NOTES 1-4 - A husband can now be convicted of raping his wife: *R. v R (rape: marital exemption)*
[1991] 4 All E.R. 481, HL

**Vol 22**

**1117 Offences by one spouse against the other**
NOTE 1 - A husband can now be convicted of raping his wife: *R. v R (rape: marital exemption)* [1991] 4 All E.R. 481 HL. (See further CRIMINAL LAW, VOL 11(1) (reissue), para 515.)

**Current Service**

Check in the Noter-up volume, in the sub-section entitled Noter-up under the volume and paragraph number where there is no entry. In order to update this information completely check the Monthly Reviews contained in the other volume of the Current Service. The Monthly Reviews are cross-referenced to the main Halsbury's Laws volumes by the Cumulative Index to the Reviews at the back of the volume.

**rape**
Marital exemption -
Law Commission proposals, 92/589
validity, 92/54

The Monthly Reviews are arranged according to a running paragraph sequence and paragraph 92/54 appears in November 1991 where there is an entry as follows:

**92/54 Rape - marital exemption - validity of exemption ........**

R. v R (rape: marital exemption) [1991] 4 All ER 481 (House of Lords: LORDS KEITH of KINKEL BRANDON of OAKWOOD, GRIFFITHS, ACKNER and LOWRY). Decision of Court of Appeal [1991] 2 All ER 257 reaffirmed.

**NOTE:** Although it is difficult to work your way through the updating service to Halsbury's Laws, it is worth persevering, as it frequently proves to be one of the most up to date sources of information.

### 5) LAW REPORTS INDEXES

i) **All England Law Reports Index 1936-1989**

**CRIMINAL LAW**
Rape
Husband and wife

Three cases appear of which the most recent is R. v O'Brien [1974] **3** 663, Crown Ct.

**Cumulative Tables and Index 1990-91**

**CRIMINAL**
Rape
Husband and wife -
Marital exemption

Three cases appear:

R. v C (rape: marital exemption) [1991] **1** 755, Crown Ct

R. v R (rape: marital exemption) [1991] **2** 257, CA

R. v R (rape: marital exemption) [1991] **4** 481, HL

R. v J (rape: marital exemption) [1991] **1** 759, Crown Ct.

**Current Tables and Index 1992 - Issue 2**

No entry

ii) **Law Reports Index**

**Red Index 1981-1990**

**CRIME**
**Sexual offences**
*Rape*

No entry

**HUSBAND AND WIFE**

No entry

**Red Index 1991**

**CRIME**
**Sexual offences**
*Rape*

**Reg. v R (Rape: Marital Exemption)** Owen J. [1991] 1 All E.R. 747

**Reg. v R** C.A. [1991] 2 W.L.R. 1065
H.L. (E.) [1991] 3 W.L.R. 767

**Reg. v C (Rape: Marital Exemption)** Simon Brown J. [1991] 1 All E.R. 755

**Reg. v J (Rape: Marital Exemption)** Rougier J. [1991] 1 All E.R. 759

**Pink Index 1992**

No entry under:

**CRIME**
**Sexual offences**
*Rape*

or **HUSBAND AND WIFE**

6) **DAILY LAW REPORTS INDEX**

Check the keyword index in the annual and quarterly parts under "rape". Abstracts of all three recent cases can be found. A database search reveals that a recent case on the subject - N v N Times, August 19, 1991 - has also been reported.

**NOTE:** Of the hard copy sources, the Digest is the least up-to-date source. The Daily Law Reports Index is the most up-to-date source. For commentary on these cases a search of the Legal Journals Index database reveals 20 articles including material on the Law Commission Working Paper on this topic.

7) **LAWTEL**

The LAWTEL indexing structure is as follows:

Crime
sexual offences
rape
Defences to rape
Marriage - husband and wife

A LAWTEL search reveals all the cases found in the other sources plus N v N Times, August 18, 1991

8) **LEXIS**

A LEXIS search reveals 25 references, but not N v N.

B) **Have there been any recent cases on the availability of the writ ne exeat regno?**

This example has been included as it requires you to use *The Digest*.

## CHECK

### 1) BOOKS

To find a definition

**Dictionary of Law - Curzon**

***ne exeat regno.*** That he shall not leave the kingdom. Writ restraining a person's leaving the realm, used in the case of political offenders, and later debtors where there was probable cause to believe that they were about to leave the country. See for a review of the law, Felton v Callis [1969] 1 QB 200; Al Nahkel for Contracting and Trading Ltd v Lowe [1986] QB 235

Other Dictionaries, such as Blacks and Mozley and Whiteley also contain definitions

**Supreme Court Practice (White Book - 1991 ed)**

The Index/Tables appear in Volume 3

**Writ ne exeat regno**
Mareva injunction, 29/1/23
money judgment, enforcement of, 45/1/37

These references refer you to the appropriate order and rule. Order 29 informs us that the writ ne exeat regno cannot be issued for the purpose of enforcing a Mareva injunction. Ord.45/1/37 explains when this writ may be used and gives all the relevant cases.

For completely up to date information check the Third Cumulative Supplement (up to date to 31 July 1991) which contains no further information.

### 2) ENCYCLOPAEDIAS

To find a definition of ne exeat regno check *Halsburys Laws Consolidated Index 1990*

WRIT
ne exeat regno, **3(1)**, 329n[11]; **8,** 995, 1246

3) **THE DIGEST**

**Consolidated Index 1992**

no entries under
**WRIT**
**PREROGATIVE ORDER**
**PRACTICE**

entry under
**WRIT OF *NE EXEAT REGNO***
alien, against **2** *Aliens* 1029

entry under
**EQUITY** *See NE EXEAT REGNO*

entry under
***NE EXEAT REGNO***
cases where writ available
account **20** *Eqy* 4929-4931
debt liquidated, due and payable
due and payable **20** *Eqy* 4922-4924
money payable by future date under order of court **20** *Eqy* 4925
equitable debt
equitable demand, only for **20** *Eqy* 4926,4927
evasion of service of process **20** *Eqy* 4919
generally **20** *Eqy* 4918
Judicature Act, 1908 **20** *Eqy* 4921
recovery of debt endangered **20** *Eqy* 4920
restriction to cases within Debtors Act **20** *Eqy* 4914-4916, 4917

Most cases were in the 19th century with one in 1968

**Continuation Volume H**

Under Vol 20 - Equity:

**4917a** *Ne exeat regno*
AL NAHKEL FOR CONTRACTING AND TRADING LTD v LOWE [1986] 1 All E.R. 729; [1986] 2 W.L.R. 317

Consd: Allied Arab Bank Ltd v Hajjar [1987] 3 All E.R. 739

**Cumulative Supplement 1992**

**4917a** AL NAHKEL FOR CONTRACTING AND TRADING LTD v LOWE (1986) See Continuation Vol H

Consd: Allied Arab Bank Ltd v Hajjar [1987] 3 All E.R. 739

**NOTE:** Use of this writ has been revived recently. If you need further information for your principal you could check Legal Journals Index where there is likely to be learned analysis of the revival of this writ which will cite and discuss all the relevant cases. A search of the database using "exeat" and "regno" reveals 8 articles.

### 4) LEXIS

A LEXIS search reveals that there were no cases in the database before 1968 but the expression had occurred in 14 cases decided after that date.

## 3.5.4 Finding cases interpreting legislation

You may be asked to find out whether there have been any cases on a particular piece of legislation.

**Have there been any cases under s.395 Companies Act 1985? (Certain charges invalid if not registered).**

This problem has been included because it illustrates the difficulties involved in trying to trace legislation which is prospectively altered by a later act.

## CHECK

### 1) BOOKS

The CCH *British company law and practice* has 10 index entries under s.395. These references lead to a wealth of case law, including that decided under earlier legislation. However, if we are being literal, it is not always obvious whether a particular decision has actually been decided under this section or not, but this is a quick route to much relevant primary material. Note also that the Cumulative Index/New Developments section has a table of destinations and derivations for the 1985 and 1989 Acts and this tells you that ss.395-408 of the 1985 Act are affected by ss.93-104 of the 1989 Act. It is therefore necessary to go to the primary sources to ascertain the correct position.

### 2) HALSBURY'S STATUTES

**Tables of Statutes and General Index 1991-92**

Companies Act 1985 **8**, 104

Go to Volume 8 Companies which now appears in its 1991 reissue and find the relevant section of the Act. The annotated notes following the section will give details of any cases. There are several cases mentioned. Note that the annotation also states that "new ss.395-420 applying throughout Great Britain are inserted by the Companies Act 1989, ss.93-104 as from a day to be appointed". Go to s.93 of the Companies Act 1989 in the same volume at p.852 and check the annotations to discover whether this section has been brought into force. The following information is given:

"Up to 1 December 1990 no order had been made under s.215(2) post" (the enabling section).

To update this information, check the Cumulative Supplement 1992, which is up to date to 1st January 1992. The Vol.8 (1991 Reissue Companies) section (a noter-up of the 1991 reissue of Vol.8) has nothing under Companies Act 1985 s.395 and nothing for Companies Act 1989 s.93.

To update this information look in the loose leaf *Noter-Up Service* printed on the blue pages. This is set out in the same way as the Cumulative Supplement ie in the same order as the volumes. Find Volume 8 and the note which covers s.215 which appears as follows:-

**COMPANIES**
**Volume 8 (1991 Reissue)**
Section 215

891-892n
"*Orders under this section.* Add: the Companies Act 1989 (Commencement No.9 and Transitional and Saving Provisions) Order 1991 SI 1991/488; ...... [details of other commencement orders] bringing into force provisions of this Act not printed in this title etc"

### 3) CURRENT LAW LEGISLATION CITATOR

**Current Law Legislation Citator 1972-1988**

This is arranged chronologically and within each year by chapter number. Turn to the 1985 section - the Companies Act 1985 is c.6.

Find s.395 and 2 recent cases are mentioned which do not appear in *Halsburys Statutes*.

**Current Law Legislation Citator 1989/91**

6. Companies Act 1985
   s.395, see *Weldtech Equipment, Re* [1991] BCC 16, Hoffman J.

**Current Law Monthly Digest June [1992] 6 C.L.**

Statute Citator
1985

**6. Companies Act 1985**
   ss. 395, 404, see *Exeter Trust v Screenways* [1991] BCC 477, C.A.

**Noter-Up**

To update this research, check in the Citator Noter-Up in the Service File to Current Law Statutes Annotated, which has the entry

**6. Companies Act 1985**
   ss. 395, 401 see *Screenways, Re*, *The Independent*, June 15, 1991, C.A.

**NOTE:** The different names given by the sources to the same case and also an incorrect Independent reference!

4) **LAW REPORTS INDEXES**

i) **Law Reports Index**

Check section entitled *Statutes Judicially Considered.*

**Red Index 1981-1990**

No entry

**Red Index 1991**

No entry

**Pink Index 1992**

No entry

ii) **All England Law Reports Consolidated Tables and Index 1936-1989**

This has a section in Volume 1 Tables entitled *Statutes Considered* which is arranged alphabetically by title of the Act but remember that the references given are only to All E.R.

There are no entries under s.395 Companies Act 1985 in 1946-1989 Index, Cumulative Tables and Index 1990-91, and Current Tables and Index 1992 - Issue 2.

**NOTE**: That these indexes include Statutory Instruments, R.S.C., other Conventions and EEC legislation which has been judicially considered.

5) **LEGAL JOURNALS INDEX**

Check the legislation index under Companies Act 1985 s.395 which reveals one item each for 1986, 1987, 1988, 1989, two for 1990 and one for 1991. Alternatively, a database search will yield the same result.

6) **DAILY LAW REPORTS INDEX**

Check the legislation index under Companies Act 1985 s.395 or search the database.

7) **LAWTEL**

This can be searched by section of an Act and reveals four cases on this section, and answers to four Research Bureau questions.

8) **LEXIS**

This can be searched by section of an Act and reveals twenty one cases and is therefore easily the most comprehensive source. Some were both recent and unreported. The strategy used was:

Companies w/5 1985 w/15 395

## 3.5.5 Finding cases interpreting statutory instruments.

**Have there been any cases interpreting the Asbestos Regulations 1969?**

## CHECK

1) **LAW REPORTS INDEXES**

i) **Law Reports Index**

Check in the section entitled "Statutory Instruments Etc Judicially Considered" towards the back of the volume

**Red Index 1981-90**

**Asbestos Regulations 1969** (S.I. 1969 no.690)
regs. 2(3), 5(1), 8(1): Reg. v AI Industrial Products Ltd [1987] I.C.R. 418 CA.

regs. 3(1)(2), 5(1)(2): Nurse v Morganite Crucible Ltd [1989] A.C. 692; [1989] 2 W.L.R. 82; [1989] I.C.R. 15 (HL)E.

**Red Index 1991**

No entry

**Pink Index 1992**

No entry

Consult the index in later weekly parts of W.L.R. to bring your research up to date.

ii) **All England Law Reports Consolidated Tables and Index 1936-1989**

Towards the back of Volume 1: Tables is an index entitled "Statutes Considered" which is divided into alphabetical sections, section A being Public General Statutes. Work your way through this to Section L-Regulations where you will find the Asbestos Regulations 1969 at p.850

Asbestos Regulations 1969

| | |
|---|---|
| reg 2(3) | [1987] **2** 368 |
| regs 3,5,8(1),9,15 | [1989] **1** 113 |
| reg 5(1) | [1987] **2** 368 |
| reg 8(1) | [1987] **2** 368 |

**Cumulative Tables and Index 1990-91**

No entry

**Current Tables and Index 1992 - Issue 2**

No entry

Consult the indexes published irregularly during the year to bring your research up to date.

2) **LEXIS**

A search of "Asbestos Regulations" reveals nine cases, one of which is fairly recent and is unreported.

3) **CURRENT LAW**

This notes cases interpreting statutory instruments each month under the relevant subject headings. Thus cases interpreting the Asbestos Regulations will be found in the Health and Safety at Work section.

4) **LEGAL JOURNALS INDEX**

A database search reveals eight relevant articles.

5) **DAILY LAW REPORTS INDEX**

A database search reveals a relevant case.

# Chapter 4: LEGISLATION

Though researching case law is complicated enough, you will find that gaining an understanding of the legislative base of a subject area is more complicated still. As with case law, there are tools which will help and these will be discussed in some detail. Also, legislation can be broken down into distinct categories. For example, there is a simple distinction to be drawn between statutes and subordinate legislation.

Statutes as enacted provide the bare bones of legislation which is then generally fleshed out by subordinate or delegated legislation usually statutory instruments. However ministerial circulars are becoming almost as important in their effects as statutory instruments, as are Inland Revenue Statements of Practice and extra-statutory concessions in the field of tax law.

## 4.1 Statutes

Most statute law will have been initiated by the government of the day and having been granted the Royal Assent, included within the category known as Public General Acts. Each of these Acts is numbered sequentially within a given calendar year with a "chapter number". This is a hangover from the days when the legislation of any particular year was regarded as a continuous book and each act was a constitutional chapter. Some works, such as the *Current Law Legislation Citator* arrange statutes by chapter number, instead of alphabetical order, within a given calendar year.

It is most usual to cite an Act of Parliament by its short title and calendar year. For example the Theft Act 1968. More formally and more generally in older works, Acts are referred to by regnal year and chapter number. The needless complexity of using regnal years was abolished in 1962, having been abandoned for purposes of the publication of the annual volumes of Public General Acts in 1940. It will still be encountered from time to time. Thus, the Hire Purchase Act 1954 is properly cited as:

2 & 3 Eliz. 2 c.51

which is to say it is chapter 51 of the statutes passed in the second and third year of the reign of Queen Elizabeth the Second. Legal historians might even notice a preference for the latinised form. Thus "Jacobi, decimo; et Scotiae quadragesimo quinto" might be less poetically but more economically expressed as 1612.

Various works are available which will convert regnal years into calendar years including *Osborn's Concise Law Dictionary* and *Lawyers Law Books*. The *Oxford Companion to English Law* is one of the more surprising but perhaps one of the more accessible of these sources.

The official definitive text of the statute law made within a given calendar year is published in a series by HMSO known as *Public General Acts and Measures*. The Measures are the *Measures of the General Synod of the Church of England*, there being an established church in England.

Some legislation is local in effect. The introduction of local legislation is a familiar device for extending the powers of individual local authorities for example. Such Acts have chapter numbers in roman numerals. Less frequently, one might come across personal legislation. Chapter numbers are in italic roman. Though limited in their application, these are all statutes but they can only be

found in the series known as *Local and Personal Acts*. There is an *Index to Local and Personal Acts* 1801-1947, a supplementary volume covering 1948-1966 and annual issues thereafter.

Remember that it is essential to establish whether a given legislative provision is in force, and the date upon which it came into force. A statute will probably indicate that various sections or schedules will come into force on either a date specified, or on a date to be appointed by a minister. In the latter case, commencement orders will usually have to be laid, though in certain circumstances it may be by notice in the London Gazette.

### 4.1.1 Statutory sources

There are various sources available for tracing modern statute law.

#### i. Law Reports Statutes

Well known in law libraries, this is a reproduction of the so-called "Queen's Printers copy" - the text published by HMSO, referred to *ante* and known as the *Public General Acts and Measures*. Reliance on this source is sufficient provided that you are content with the text of an Act exactly as it received the Royal Assent. However in most cases you will want annotations describing the effect of the legislation, and at least an indication of the ways in which it has been subsequently amended or repealed. It is surprising how often the bare text of an Act is of but limited value. Even very straightforward and simple pieces of legislation are the subject of repeals, amendments, commencement orders, regulations and judicial interpretation. On all these matters the text as originally published is silent.

#### ii. Halsbury's Statutes

The fourth edition which commenced publication in 1985 is now almost complete. Volumes are arranged in subject order giving a text as amended plus annotations as the law stands at the date on which the volume in question went to press. Statutes awaiting incorporation in reissues of the bound volumes are published in looseleaf format in the *Current Statutes Service*. In addition, there is a *Cumulative Supplement* and *Noter-Up* which includes references to those volumes in the third edition which have not yet been superseded by the fourth.

A possible source of confusion when using this work is that its design approaches a codification of the law, and a single Act might be divided amongst several titles. Also, specifically Scottish legislation is excluded. Each title does have a subject index, and there is a separate reasonably comprehensive index for the set as a whole.

#### iii. Current Law Statutes Annotated

Beginning in 1948, this series gives the text of all Public General Acts together with certain explanatory notes and annotations. Statutes of the current year are issued first as grey paper copies (unannotated) and secondly on white paper (with annotations) both in looseleaf form, before bound volumes appear. From 1992, the service has included all Private Acts and also now contains a table showing progress of Bills and a citator giving consolidations of legislation.

iv. **STATUTES IN FORCE**

This work is published by HMSO and is a well-intentioned attempt to create a comprehensive looseleaf set of statutes which can be readily brought up to date as they are amended. It is unannotated and the amendments are not produced very quickly. It cannot be recommended for current research questions.

v. **LAWTEL**

LAWTEL does not provide any text but does offer a convincing skeletal arrangement. It is possible to identify repeals, amendments and commencements and regulations made under an Act, for the period 1984 to date. This is of outstanding value for complex pieces of legislation like the Insolvency Acts.

vi. **LEXIS**

LEXIS should hold the full amended text of all legislation in force, but no extra editorial matter is added in the way of footnotes. Some skillful use of LEXIS will enable you to trace the effect of prospective amendments.

## 4.2 Research using statutes

### 4.2.1 The status of an Act

It is always necessary to check whether the text you happen to have in front of you is the law currently in force. You need to know whether any section or schedule has been amended or repealed by later legislation.

i. **HALSBURY'S STATUTES**

If the Act is in a 3rd or 4th edition volume all amendments and repeals up to the date of publication for each volume are included in the text and noted. Later amendments and repeals for all volumes, and for the *Current Statutes Service*, are noted in the *Cumulative Supplement* which is issued annually. There is a looseleaf *Noter-up* which deals with amendments and repeals since the publication of the most recent *Cumulative Supplement*. The *Noter-up* is divided into two sections: 4th edition and *Current Statutes Service* and unreplaced 3rd edition volumes.

ii. **CURRENT LAW LEGISLATION CITATOR**

Statutes are listed chronologically (by year and then chapter number) noting amendments and repeals. The volume covering 1947 to 1971 is actually called the *Current Law Statute Citator*. The bound volumes are kept up to date by looseleaf pages issued with *Current Law Statutes Annotated* and the *Statute Citator* section in *Current Law Monthly Digest*.

iii. **CHRONOLOGICAL TABLE OF THE STATUTES**

This work is published every two years by HMSO. It lists every statute enacted since 1235, in chronological order, noting repeals and amendments. Thus, it is a much more complete work than the *Current Law Legislation Citator*. There is also a separate table of Local and Personal Acts showing amendments and repeals since 1973.

iv. **LAWTEL**

For statutes enacted after 1984 it is possible to rely on LAWTEL to give an indication of how the original Act has been amended or repealed. It will also show what statutory instruments have been made, and their effects.

v. **LEXIS**

It should be possible to rely on LEXIS to provide a current statement of the statute law in force.

### 4.2.2 Commencement of Acts

Statutes may not come into force on the date they receive the Royal Assent. The date of Royal Assent appears in square brackets at the end of the long title. Usually but not invariably, the last section of an Act will give its "commencement and extent". Different sections and schedules may come into force on different dates. There are three possibilities for each section or schedule:

- it will come into force on a stated date, say two months after the Royal Assent;
- the Minister is given powers to bring it into force with commencement orders;
- there is no special commencement provision, so it is in force from the date it receives Royal Assent.

You can use the following sources to establish whether an Act is in force.

i. **IS IT IN FORCE?**

Acts are listed alphabetically within each calender year giving details of commencements and repeals. It covers those statutes passed since 1961. It is published annually as part of *Halsbury's Statutes* and is updated by looseleaf pages in the *Noter-up*.

ii. **CURRENT LAW STATUTES ANNOTATED**

Looseleaf pages are issued containing a table of legislation not yet in force, which can be updated by the monthly issues of *Current Law*. The Service File has included a section containing the full text of all Commencement Orders since 1992.

iii. **CURRENT LAW**

This contains a cumulative list of "dates of commencement - Statutes" for the current year. These are the dates a Minister has appointed on which legislation will come into force.

iv. **HALSBURY'S STATUTORY INSTRUMENTS**

In the looseleaf service volumes there is an alphabetical *List of Commencement and Appointed Day Orders* specifying the commencement and operation of statutes for the current year. The instruments listed are those which are noted in the *Monthly Survey* in the service binder.

v. **BOOKS AND JOURNALS**

Specialist books particularly looseleaf encyclopaedias are always worth consulting, since they usually take the form of a commentary plus appropriate statutory materials brought together for convenience and constantly updated.

The *New Law Journal*, *Solicitor's Journal*, and the *Law Society's Gazette* are three of the weekly journals which list statutory instruments including commencement orders.

vi. **DAILY LIST OF GOVERNMENT PUBLICATIONS**

This is a list of new HMSO publications of the day. The last section contains details of all new statutory instruments published, including commencement orders.

vii. **LAWTEL**

For statutes enacted after 1983 LAWTEL is a particularly helpful source because it is reliably up to date.

viii. **LEXIS**

Statutes can be found in a separate file within the ENGGEN library. It can be searched for "date in force" for any section of any Act.

### 4.2.3 Tracing statute law by subject

Most of the tools available for searching statute law by subject are rather blunt and tend not to go down to the level of detail involved in the production of looseleaf encyclopaedias.

i. **HALSBURY'S STATUTES**

The *Consolidated Tables and Index* to the 4th edition is the most detailed subject index available. There are also indexes in the individual subject volumes.

ii. **INDEX TO THE STATUTES**

This is a companion work to the *Chronological Table of the Statutes*, and is also published by HMSO. Its publication cycle is somewhat in arrears and the subject headings chosen rather broad. It includes a chronological table of statutes by regnal year and it also serves as an index to the **Statutes in Force**.

### iii. CURRENT LAW STATUTES ANNOTATED

Each annual bound volume has a subject index, but this is not cumulated.

### iv. CURRENT LAW

Amongst other legal developments for the month in question, this provides a digest of recent legislation, together with a cumulative subject index to date.

### v. LEXIS

The problem with searching case law by subject is the need to enter the mind of the judge. Legislation can also be searched by subject provided one can enter the mind of the legislator. It is at all times important to remember that with LEXIS you may search for occurrences of words but that this is not the same as searching by subject. There are no subject headings in LEXIS.

## 4.3 Statutory Instruments

If the legislation you are looking for is described as Orders, Regulations, Rules or Directions, or in some cases Schemes or Warrants, you are probably searching for a Statutory Instrument, or SI for short. Before 1946 these were published in a series known as *Statutory Rules and Orders.*

They are published individually by HMSO and at one time were collected into bound volumes arranged in subject order, but this process took so long that as from 1961 they have been published in numerical order but are still very late in publication.

The SI's in force and as amended on 31 December 1948 were published in subject order in a work entitled *The Statutory Rules & Orders and Statutory Instruments Revised.*

As there are Acts which are local or personal in effect, so there are SI's of local or personal effect, and these are not reprinted in bound volumes. They can normally be obtained from the local authority or other public body responsible for their promotion.

Tracing older SI's can be a problem. Instruments made between 1922 and 1947 are to be found in the Public Record Office, but apparently no complete collection of those made between 1890 and 1921 has been traced. However, the practitioner is chiefly interested in those SI's in force or only recently revoked.

SI's are known by title and year of publication eg:

*The Notices to Quit (Prescribed Information) Regulations 1980*

or by year and running number

S.I. 1980 No. 1624

### 4.3.1 Finding SI's

#### i. HALSBURY'S STATUTORY INSTRUMENTS

This is a subject guide to SI's in force. The series of black volumes is in the course of being replaced by grey volumes which have been revised and modernised with changes in the subject headings being used. Individual volumes are re-issued from time to time. Each volume notes whether an existing SI has been revoked, repealed, superseded, lapsed or spent, correct at the date of publication. There is an annual index covering the work as a whole, and indexes for the individual titles will be found in the appropriate volumes.

You will soon discover that many of the SI's recorded in this work are only printed in summary form or merely noted. The publishers say that it is impractical to produce and keep up to date any publication containing the full text of every SI in force.

The work is kept up to date by two service volumes. Volume 1 contains a *Users Guide*; a *Title-Key* which sets out the titles in the black volumes and the corresponding titles in the new grey volumes and vice versa; a *Chronological List of Instruments* which comprises all instruments included in the main volumes and the Service which were in force on 1 January 1986. The list indicates which title each SI may be found in. A *Table of Statutes* indicates the enabling statutes under which statutory instruments dealt with in the work have effect and there is an alphabetical list of commencement and appointed day orders. In addition there is an *Annual Supplement* and a *Monthly Survey*. This is in two parts. The first part, the *Title Key*, lists new instruments, instruments revoked and amendments by subject title. The second part gives summaries of the

SI's in numerical order with an index. The *Monthly Survey* cumulates throughout the year, eventually forming the *Annual Supplement*.

Volume 2 contains the full text of selected SI's though beware as they may not always include all the schedules and tables contained in some instruments.

ii. **HALSBURY'S STATUTES**

SI's made under a given section are noted in the annotations in the main volumes. Later instruments are noted in the *Cumulative Supplement* and *Noter-up*.

iii. **CURRENT LAW LEGISLATION CITATOR**

This notes SI's made under sections of Acts but only gives the year and number of the instrument.

iv. **INDEX TO GOVERNMENT ORDERS**

This is the "official" index and lists enabling statutes under subject headings, together with details of the SI's which have been made. There is a chronological table of enabling statutes at the front of the work giving the subject headings under which they are to be found. This index is published every two years with a noting up supplement in alternate years.

v. **LIST OF STATUTORY INSTRUMENTS**

This is published monthly with an annual cumulation, which is called the *Annual List of Statutory Instruments*. Details of each SI are given under broad subject headings. There is a detailed, cumulative alphabetical index. There is also a cumulative numerical list of SI's with their subject headings indicating the month in which they were issued.

vi. **CURRENT LAW YEARBOOK**

Each of these annual volumes provides an alphabetical table of the SI's made each year arranged under subject headings.

### 4.3.2 Tracing recent SI's

*Current Law* notes new SI's issued each month under the appropriate subject headings. The *New Law Journal*, *Solicitor's Journal*, and the *Law Society's Gazette* all note new SI's. The most comprehensive listing is to be found in the HMSO *Daily List of Government Publications* which also gives their commencement dates.

LEXIS can be used to search for SI's as a group, or for statutes and SI's together in one file. For individual sections of Acts the "Authority" segment can be used to discover relevant SI's.

Probably LAWTEL is the most useful source for recent SI's listed under statutes and sections. It is particularly helpful because it gives the effect of each SI.

# WORKS MENTIONED

*Current Law Legislation Citator*
London, Sweet & Maxwell, 1972-

Walker, D.M.
*Oxford Companion to Law*
Oxford, O.U.P., 1980

*Public General Acts and Measures*
London, H.M.S.O., 1831-

*Index to Local and Personal Acts 1801-1847*
London, H.M.S.O., 1948
Supplementary index 1948-1966
London, H.M.S.O., 1967

*Current Law Statutes Annotated*
London, Sweet & Maxwell, 1948-

*Statutes in Force*
London, H.M.S.O., 1972-

*Chronological Table of the Statutes*
London, H.M.S.O., 1235- [current year]

*Statutory Rules and Orders and Statutory Instruments Revised*
To December 31, 1948
London, H.M.S.O., 1949-1952

*List of Statutory Instruments*
London, H.M.S.O.
Annual

*Current Law Yearbook*
London, Sweet & Maxwell, 1947-
Annual

# Legal Research Using Statutes

## Practical Examples

It is recommended that you work through these problems using the books listed as this should give you some idea of the steps involved in researching the problems. Merely reading through these examples will only serve to confuse!

The problems are keyed into the relevant paragraph numbers in the text.

## 4.2.1 Ascertaining whether a section of an Act is in force

**Is s.2 of the Consumer Protection Act 1987 on liability for defective products in force?**

## CHECK

1) **IS IT IN FORCE? 1991**

This arranges statutes alphabetically by title within the year.
It indicates that s.2 came into force on 1st March 1988 by SI 1987/1680.

2) **CURRENT LAW LEGISLATION CITATOR**

In this instance it is not so helpful, as it merely gives the numbers of the commencement orders without stating when the sections came into force.

## 4.2.2 Ascertaining whether an Act has been repealed

**Has the Prevention of Fraud (Investments) Act 1958 been repealed and, if so, by what later legislation?**

## CHECK

1) **HALSBURY'S STATUTES**

**Tables of Statutes and General Index 1991-92**

The *Alphabetical List of Statutes* does not contain the Prevention of Fraud (Investments) Act 1958. Neither is it in the Chronological List of Statutes. We can therefore safely assume that it has been repealed.

2) **IS IT IN FORCE 1991?**

This source only gives details of repeals and commencement of Acts since 1966, so will not cover the Prevention of Fraud (Investments) Act as it was passed in 1958.

3) **CURRENT LAW LEGISLATION CITATOR**

**Current Law Legislation Citator 1972-1988**

**45. Prevention of Fraud (Investments) Act 1958**
repealed: 1986, c.60, sch.17.

This refers to schedule 17 of the Financial Services Act 1986.
The Schedule lists all the repeals and revocations made by the Financial Services Act. Unfortunately this schedule is being brought into force gradually by commencement orders. In order to discover whether the Prevention of Fraud (Investments) Act is repealed, it is necessary to pursue alternative methods of research.

**Current Law Legislation Citator 1989/91**

No entry

4) **CHRONOLOGICAL TABLE OF THE STATUTES**

This tells us that the Prevention of Fraud (Investments) Act 1958 is prospectively repealed by the Financial Services Act 1986 (c.60), s.212(3), sch.17 but does not give a date.

5) **LEXIS**

Some advanced searching on *LEXIS* in the STAT file can be relied upon to indicate amendments and prospective amendments to existing legislation. However, for this type of enquiry it is necessary to be reasonably accomplished in *LEXIS* searching and it is not necessarily either the most cost or time effective method of proceeding. Since the STAT file makes each section of an Act a separate document it is most efficient when determining whether an individual section has been amended or repealed.

6) **LAWTEL**

A LAWTEL search reveals that SI 1989/1583 repeals the remainder of the Prevention of Fraud (Investments) Act 1958 not so far repealed but for this it is necessary to know that the Financial Services Act 1986 is the starting point .

**NOTE**: A good way of double checking whether you have reached the correct answer is to ring the relevant section of the Department of Trade and Industry dealing with the Financial Services Act and provided you speak to the right person, they should be able to give you information far more quickly.

### 4.2.3 Tracing statute law by subject

Two problems are illustrated for this exercise.

A)i) **Has there been any legislation relating to pyramid selling schemes? Has the legislation been judicially considered?**

There may have been either or both primary and secondary legislation.

PRIMARY LEGISLATION

## CHECK

1) **HALSBURY'S STATUTES**

**Table of Statutes and General Index 1991-92**

Refers to Volume 47, 204
which is the Fair Trading Act 1973 s.119 and deals with the power to make regulations relating to trading schemes

SECONDARY LEGISLATION

## CHECK

1) **HALSBURY'S STATUTORY INSTRUMENTS**

**Consolidated Index 1991-92**

Pyramid selling schemes:
general regulations....S(1989/2195)

The letter S refers to instruments dealt with in the Annual Supplement which is contained within Volume 1 of the Service Volumes. Such instruments may be traced using the Chronological List of Instruments also contained in Service Volume 1 which will indicate the relevant title in the Annual Supplement

SI 1989
2195 Pyramid Selling Schemes Regulations 1989......Sale of Goods

Reference to the Title Key also contained in Service Volume 1 links Sale of Goods to Volume 17

**Annual Supplement**

Vol. 17 Sale of Goods at page 463 contains a summary of the Regulations. Note at the end of the abstract that these Regulations have been amended as of 1 March 1990 by SI 1990/150 "to correct errors".

**ii) Has the legislation been judicially considered?**

## CHECK

### 1) LAW REPORTS INDEXES

i) **Law Reports Index 1971-1980; 1981-1990**

Check under Statutes Judicially Considered and Statutory Instruments Judicially Considered.

No entry

**Red Index 1991**

No entry

**Pink Index 1992**

No entry

ii) **All England Law Reports Cumulative Tables and Index 1990-91**

Check under Statutes Considered: A: Public General Statutes and L: Regulations.

No entry

**Current tables and Index 1992 - Issue 2**

No entry

### 2) CURRENT LAW LEGISLATION CITATOR

**Current Law Legislation Citator 1972-1988**

No entry

**Current Law Legislation Citator 1989/91**
Statutory Instruments Affected 1989-91

1989
2195 amended 90/150

3) **LEXIS**

By selecting the STATIS file in LEXIS - the combined statutes and statutory instruments file - it is possible to retrieve all documents which include the expression "pyramid selling".

4) **LAWTEL**

LAWTEL reveals that the Pyramid Selling Schemes (Amendment) Regulations 1990, SI 1990/150, amend the Pyramid Selling Schemes Regulations 1989, SI 1989/2195 which themselves revoke SI 1973/1740.

NOTE: This is the most up to date source for this problem.

**B) Has there been any recent legislation on planning consent regarding hazardous substances?**

There may have been either or both primary and secondary legislation

# CHECK

## PRIMARY LEGISLATION

1) **HALSBURYS STATUTES**

**Table of Statutes and General Index 1991-92**

Planning:

No entry

Town and country planning:

No entry

**Hazardous substances**
Consent -
application for -
regulations **46**, 1112

Volume 46 (1990 reissue) p.1112

Planning (Hazardous Substances) Act 1990

**7 Applications for hazardous substances consent**

The notes section states that up to 1 August 1990 no regulations had been made under this section, and refers to s.40 of the Act which provides for the Secretary of State to make regulations.

**Cumulative Supplement 1991**

Volume 46
**Planning (Hazardous Substances) Act 1990 (c.10)**
**112 Section 7**

States that various amendments are made by the Environmental Protection Act 1990. Regulations may make provision for payment of a fee for applications for hazardous substances consent.

s.40 No entry

**Cumulative Supplement 1992**

Adds nothing to the information given in the 1991 Supplement.

**NOTE:** The Index to the Service is now contained in the Table of Statutes and General Index 1991-92. Check in the Service Index at p.1102

Hazardous substances

No entry

Town and Country Planning

No entry

This Index is only up-to-date to July 1991, so check the Noter-Up.

Volume 46
Town and Country Planning
s.7 No entry
s.40 No entry

From this, it would seem that there have been no regulations, but check the secondary sources.

## SECONDARY SOURCES

**HALSBURYS STATUTORY INSTRUMENTS**
Consolidated Index 1991-92

Hazardous substances

No entry

Town and country planning

No entry

This index is only up-to-date to October 1991

For more recent regulations, check:

**Service Volumes (Vol.1)**
Annual Cumulative Supplement 1991

Vol.20 Town and Country Planning

No entry

**Monthly Survey/Key and Index (1 January 1991 to 30 April 1992)**

Town and Country Planning
Vol.20 (Grey Volume)

1992/656 Planning (Hazardous Substances) Regulations 1992
1992/725 Planning (Hazardous Substances) Act 1990 (Commencement and Transitional Provisions) Order 1992

The Monthly Survey-Summaries section in the same looseleaf volume contains summaries of these two SIs.

# Legal research using statutory instruments

### Practical Examples

It is recommended that you work through these problems using the books listed as this should give you some idea of the steps involved in researching the problems. Merely reading through these examples will only serve to confuse.

## 4.3.1 Finding statutory instruments by subject

**Have there been any recent SIs relating to the irradiation of food? Has there been any comment on these regulations?**

## CHECK

1) **HALSBURY'S STATUTORY INSTRUMENTS**

**Consolidated Index 1991-1992**

Food
    irradiation, control of .. S (1990/2490)

To check whether there have been further regulations

**Service Volume 1**
Annual Cumulative Supplement 1991
Vol 8 Food
    Chronological List of Instruments
    1990/2490 Food (Control of Irradiation) Regulations 1990 289

A summary of the regulations is given on p.289

To bring your research up to date check Monthly Survey Key and Index under FOOD, Vol 8 where new instruments, revocations and amendments are listed. There do not appear to have been any more recent regulations.

2) **TABLE OF GOVERNMENT ORDERS**

**NOTE**: This is only up to date to 31st December, 1987 with a Noter-Up to 31st August, 1988.

**Has there been any comment on these regulations?**

## CHECK

**LEGAL JOURNALS INDEX**

There are four articles on the subject of food irradiation.

## 4.3.2 Finding statutory instruments under an Act

**Have any SIs been laid under s.9 Company Directors Disqualification Act 1986 relating to matters for determining the unfitness of directors?**

## CHECK

1) **CURRENT LAW LEGISLATION CITATOR**

**Current Law Legislation Citator 1972-1988**

No entry

**Current Law Legislation Citator 1989/91**

No entry

**Monthly Digest June [1992] 6 C.L.**

No entry

2) **HALSBURY'S STATUTES**

Find the relevant volume by checking the Table of Statutes and General Alphabetical List of Statutes

Company Directors Disqualification Act 1986 **8(S)**, Companies 1

Turn to Current Statutes Service Vol 8 Companies where you will only find the Foreign Corporations Act 1991. The Alphabetical List of Statutes does not include the Company Directors Disqualification Act 1986.

Go to Vol.8. This is a 1991 reissue and is up to date to 1 October 1990. The Table of Statutes lists the Act, at page 781. Check the relevant section and it states that up to 1 October 1990 no orders have been laid under this section.

**Cumulative Supplement 1991**

No entry

**Noter-up**

No entry

**Cumulative Supplement 1992**

No entry

3) **HALSBURY'S STATUTORY INSTRUMENTS**

This is a more complicated method of attacking the problem and it is not to be recommended unless the two previous sources are unavailable.

Check in the Service Volume in the section entitled **Table of Statutes**

This lists enabling Acts under which SIs dealt with in *Halsbury's Statutory Instruments* were made. In fact, no entry appears under s.9 Company Directors Disqualification Act.

You can of course check the general subject of Companies in the hope of finding something.

4) **INDEX TO GOVERNMENT ORDERS IN FORCE ON 31 DECEMBER 1987**

Look up the Act in the *Chronological Table* which is printed on green pages, in the A-K index volume.

**NOTE**: This Index is only current to 31 December 1987.

No entry

## 4.3.3 Finding out whether statutory instruments have been amended

**Has the Restrictive Trade Practices Services Order been amended?**

## CHECK

**HALSBURY'S STATUTORY INSTRUMENTS**

**Consolidated Index 1991/92**

Restrictive Trade Practices:
restrictive agreements:
supply and acquisition of services ***20***, *267, (1976/98)*

The reference is given in italics which means that the SI appears in the new grey Volume 20 under the subject heading "Trade and Industry Part 1B - Monopolies and Restrictive Trade Practices".

The SI referred to is the 1976 Order. It seems likely that this order which is now 15 years old, will have been amended. Therefore check the Service Volumes

**Service Volumes**

Annual Supplement
Vol. 20 Trade and Industry Part 1B.

1989/1082 Restrictive Trade Practices (Services) (Amendment) Order 1989

**NOTE:** The text of this Order does not appear in the Supplement

Monthly Survey - Key and Index

No amendments or revocations appear here

# Chapter 5: REFERENCE WORKS

There are a number of basic reference sources to which the legal practitioner has frequent recourse. It is beyond the scope of a guide of this kind to describe all the sources which might be used at some stage, even those of a general character. This is an introduction to the main works and services of legal reference with the widest practical application.

## 5.1 Encyclopaedias

As has been noted already, *Halsbury's Laws of England* is an excellent general encyclopaedia. The current edition is the 4th and it is complete in 56 volumes. It is arranged alphabetically by topic and gives a comprehensive outline of each subject of law, with copious footnotes detailing the main legislation and cases. There are legislation, case and subject indexes to the set as well as individual indexes for each title. It is a good place to start almost any piece of legal research.

The main work is updated by an annual *Cumulative Supplement* using the same volume and paragraph numbers as the main work itself. There is also a service binder containing the *Monthly Reviews* which digest latest developments in the law by subject. These monthly issues cumulate into the *Annual Abridgement*. There is also a cumulative noter-up issued in the service binder. A *User's Guide* accompanies this work.

**SUMMARY**

**HOW TO USE HALSBURY'S LAWS**

Consolidated Index<br>
|<br>
|<br>
Main Volumes<br>
Separate subject index for each subject at back of individual vols<br>
|<br>
|<br>
Cumulative Supplement<br>
|<br>
|<br>
|<br>
Current Service<br>
| |<br>
Monthly Review Noter Up

|<br>
Annual Abridgment

There are also many subject encyclopaedias, usually published in looseleaf form covering the main areas of legal practice eg *Encyclopaedia of Financial Services Law*, *Encyclopaedia of Banking Law*.

## 5.2 Directories

There are various directories specifically targeted at the legal practitioner as well as a whole range of works which might be of value though aimed at a wider market. Some of the more important sources are indicated below.

The *Directory of Solicitors and Barristers*, *Solicitors and Barristers Directory* and *Butterworths Law Directory and Diary* are the best sources for identifying legal practitioners in the United Kingdom. The *Legal 500* and *Chambers & Partners' Directory* are consumer's guides to the services of the largest law firms and chambers indicating their strengths and specialisations and offering some subjective comments and comparisons.

*The Martindale-Hubbell Law Directory* gives details of law firms in all jurisdictions though primarily in the United States. Also worthy of note are the *International Law List* and *Kime's International Law Directory* covering law firms in foreign jurisdictions. *Law firms in Europe* is an equivalent of the *Legal 500* for European law firms.

The best directory dealing with the courts is *Shaw's Directory of Courts in the United Kingdom*, although similar information can be found in *Hazell's Guide (Judiciary + Courts + Bar)*, which also gives comprehensive information on the Bar. A specialist directory for barristers is *Havers' Companion to the Bar.*

## 5.3 Words and phrases

It is not unusual to find that the crux of a research problem turns on the precise meaning of a word or phrase. It is true that many lawyers prefer to approach such a problem from the point of view of the substantive law relating to the area of research in question. Nevertheless, there are a number of general approaches to the question of defining the meaning of a word or phrase, and especially whether the meaning of these expressions has been judicially considered.

As well as the sources listed below it is sometimes worth checking whether an article in a journal has been written on the meaning of a particular expression. Consult *Legal Journals Index* and see what the text books on the subject have to say.

#### STROUD'S JUDICIAL DICTIONARY, 5th ed. 1986

This is an excellent "interpreting" dictionary. It contains definitions of ordinary and legal phrases as they have been interpreted by the courts and in statutes.

#### WORDS AND PHRASES LEGALLY DEFINED

This provides definitions on the basis of statutes and case law. It is updated by an annual cumulative supplement and is less comprehensive than Stroud.

### Current Law

There is a cumulative list of words and phrases considered under that heading in each monthly issue. The list is cumulated each year in the *Current Law Yearbook*.

### Halsbury's Laws of England

There is a section on words and phrases in the subject index volumes for the set, locating entries which define words and phrases in the text or in footnotes.

### Digest

This is no longer a useful source for judicial interpretations of words and phrases.

### Indexes to law reports

Many of the general series of law reports include in their indexes a list of words and phrases which have been judicially considered. The indexes to *All England Law Reports* are a good example.

### Lawtel

LAWTEL has a list of words and phrases judicially considered in the period 1980 to date.

### Lexis

It is often worthwhile to attempt a LEXIS search, especially in this instance, where it is possible to devise a very precise search strategy. In some cases, this may be the only effective means of establishing whether a judge has commented on the meaning of a particular expression.

## 5.4 Precedents

Legal practitioners frequently need precedents. A number of major works include precedents and there are various specialised collections such as *Practical Commercial Precedents*, which is written by practising lawyers and therefore has a very practical slant. Sometimes precedents can be found in specialist legal journals. There is also a general series described below.

### Encyclopaedia of Forms and Precedents

This is a comprehensive collection of the non-litigious forms and precedents required by the solicitor in every day practice. It is a companion work to *Atkin's Court Forms*. As well as the collection of forms and precedents it also provides an outline of the relevant law, and details of practice and procedure under each title.

Although completed some years ago, the 4th edition of this work is still favoured by many practitioners not the least because the 5th edition remains incomplete. There is an updating service to the 5th edition, and an annual cumulative index.

The Fourth Edition contains 24 volumes plus a *Cumulative Noter-Up* and two Service Binders contain an additional forms section which includes new or revised forms, plus a tax planning section and a current notes section which updates the notes in the main volumes and *Noter-Up* section. The Fourth Edition volumes are not being replaced sequentially by the Fifth Edition. At the beginning of the Service Binders of the Fourth and Fifth Editions there is a section entitled *Guide to the Replacement of the 4th Edition* which shows which material in the 4th edition has been replaced by the 5th edition,

The Fifth Edition has a Service Binder which includes useful information on fees, rates of tax and stamp duty information, plus a list of useful addresses for such places as the Land Registry. The format follows the same pattern in both editions. The forms are arranged by subject.

In the Fourth Edition the **heavy figures** denote the volume number and the light figures denote the page reference. If the page figures are in square brackets, this means that the reference is to the preliminary note, or if followed by the letter "n", in a footnote. If there are no brackets, the reference is to a precedent or form.

In the Fifth Edition individual volume figures without brackets denote commentary. References in the Fifth Edition are to paragraph numbers, not page numbers. Because this is a Butterworths publication, there are cross references to *Halsbury's Laws*.

A *User's Guide* accompanies this work.

## 5.5 Court forms

### ATKIN'S ENCYCLOPAEDIA OF COURT FORMS IN CIVIL PROCEEDINGS

This is a companion work to the *Encyclopaedia of Forms and Precedents* and contains forms and precedents for use in civil proceedings. The aim of *Atkins* is to provide a comprehensive collection of the necessary procedural documents for every proceeding before every court and tribunal in England and Wales that has civil jurisdiction. In addition to the relevant forms and precedents an outline of the law and, where appropriate, procedural tables are also included. This is another Butterworths publication and as far as possible the titles correspond to those used in *Halsbury's Laws* and there are cross references to it. Each title is divided into practice; procedural tables and forms.

Volume 1 *Actions* outlines general procedure in the High Court and Volume 13 *County Courts* covers general county court procedure.

Reissue volumes of the second edition keep the work up to date together with an updating service and annual index.

## 5.6 Electronic information

Although there are relatively few products available in the United Kingdom at the time of writing, it is reasonable to assume that an increasing number of reference sources will be published in electronic form in the next few years following the pattern in North America. The *Martindale Hubbell Directory* is published in hard copy, as a LEXIS library, and as a CD-ROM (Compact disk read only memory) and there has been a pilot project to issue *Simon's Taxes* in CD-ROM format.

Further developments may also be expected in the area of expert systems. These computer based systems take the lawyer stage by stage through a problem by an algorithmic path leading to an opinion on the matter in question. There is already a commercially available system on latent damage. It is necessary to suppose that the area of law dealt with can be broken down into legal rules. Clearly this methodology will not apply to every area of law. It happens that it is well suited to questions of latent damage and might be appropriate to other areas too. These systems may become more important if leading independent counsel are recruited by large law firms and accountancy practices.

Some practitioners' books are now issued with a word processing disk so that the precedents they contain can be installed in the firm's word processing system for general use.

# WORKS MENTIONED

*Encyclopaedia of Financial Services Law*
Looseleaf
London, Sweet & Maxwell

*Encyclopaedia of Banking Law*
Looseleaf
London, Butterworths

*Solicitors and Barristers Directory*
London, Waterlow Directories
Annual

*Butterworths Law Directory and Diary*
London, Butterworths
Annual

*Chambers & Partners Directory*
London, Chambers & Partners
Annual

*Directory of Solicitors and Barristers*
London, The Law Society
Annual

*Havers' Companion to the Bar*
London, Havers' Directories

*Law firms in Europe*
London, Legalease
Annual

*Legal 500*
London, Legalease
Annual

*Martindale-Hubbell Law Directory*
Summit, NJ, Martindale-Hubbell, 1868-
Annual

*International Law List*
London, Corpor Mordaunt, 1937-
Annual

*Kime's International Law Directory*
Kime, 1892-
Annual

*Shaw's Directory of Courts in the UK*
London, Shaw & Sons
Annual

*Hazell's Guide to the Judiciary and the Courts*
Henley-on-Thames, R. Hazell & Co
Annual

*Stroud, F.*
Judicial Dictionary of Words and Phrases Judicially Interpreted
5th ed.
London, Sweet & Maxwell, 1986

*Words and Phrases Legally Defined*
3rd ed.
London, Butterworths, 1988
4 vols

*Encyclopaedia of Forms and Precedents other than Court Forms*
5th ed.
London, Butterworths, 1985-
Projected 42 vols

*Atkin's Encyclopaedia of Court Forms in Civil Proceedings*
2nd ed.
London, Butterworths, 1961-
42 vols
Undergoing continuous revision

Bigelow, R.
*Computer Contracts*
Mathew Bender, 1987
3 vols

Rennie, M.
*Computer Contracts Handbook*
London, Sweet & Maxwell, 1985

## Research using forms and precedents

### Practical Examples

# Find the ACE conditions of engagement for a consulting engineer

# CHECK

1) **ENCYCLOPAEDIA OF FORMS AND PRECEDENTS 5TH ED**

**Consolidated Index 1991**



**Service Binder**
Vol. 5 Form 2 [50] - [56.3]

A Memorandum of Agreement between client and consulting engineer for report and advisory work (ACE Agreement 1) has been added.

Vol. 5 Form 3 [57] - [69]

A Memorandum of Agreement between client and consulting engineer for civil, mechanical and electrical work and for structural engineering work where an architect is not appointed by the client (ACE Agreement 2) has been added.

**NOTE**: One of the standard building contract textbooks may also contain these precedents, but Vol. 5 contains a useful set of the major building contract precedents.

## Find a precedent for donating a kidney for transplant

## CHECK

1) **ENCYCLOPAEDIA OF FORMS AND PRECEDENTS 5TH ED.**

**Consolidated Index 1991**

Check under

KIDNEY
donation for transplant, **6** 403 [481].

Paragraph 403 deals with the statutory provisions relating to the use of a body for organ transplantation or medical research and square brackets denote a precedent.

**Service Binder**

Vol. 6 para 3 Amendments have been made to the Preliminary Notes

You are acting for John Smith who wishes to install a new accounts computer and related software in his small business. He has asked you to advise upon the necessary documentation for the supply of hardware and software. One year later the software is still not working satisfactorily. Find the necessary documentation.

## CHECK

1) **TEXTBOOKS**

The following textbooks will provide some sample precedents:-

*Bigelow Computer contracts*

*Rennie Computer contracts handbook*

2) **ENCYCLOPAEDIA OF FORMS AND PRECEDENTS. 5TH ED**

Consolidated Index 1991

The Index under "Computer" contains no helpful information. There is no heading for computer contracts and the heading for "Contract" contains no information on computer contracts

3) **Legal Journals Index**

This can be very useful for obtaining background information on the problem in hand. A quick search reveals over eighty items which may be of help, eg:-

**COMPUTER CONTRACTS**
An introduction to computer contracts. By Clive Davies.
*C.L. & P. 1992, 8(2), 54-56*

**COMPUTER CONTRACTS; DISPUTE RESOLUTION**
Computer disputes: lessons and pitfalls. By Richard Stephens.
*I.C.C.L.R. 1992, 3(6), 210-213*

**COMPUTER CONTRACTS; DRAFTING**
Facilities management. (How to negotiate and draft contracts effectively). By Susan Singleton.
*C.L. & P. 1992, 8(3), 84-87*

To find the relevant form to draft a statement of claim against the manufacturer for misstatement

# CHECK

### Atkins Court Forms

Index 1992

COMPUTER CONTRACT
 fitness for purpose, **12** 123
 hardware contract -
  defective equipment, claim against supplier, **12** [156 158]

Annual Supplement 1992

Vol.12 Computers

No entry

**NOTE**: Textbooks on the subject mentioned above will probably contain relevant forms.

# APPENDIX 1 LEGAL RESEARCH: AN EXAMPLE

This is a fully worked example of the problems involved in legal research at a particular point in time. It has not been updated for the revised edition but is included to illustrate the difficulties inherent in attempting to undertake comprehensive research.

On 8 November 1984, Warner, J made an important decision in the case: Zim Properties Ltd v Proctor (Inspector of Taxes), concerning a number of complex issues in respect of capital gains tax, arising from section 22 of the Finance Act 1965, sub-sections 1, 3 and 4. Subsequently, on 19 December 1988, the Inland Revenue announced the terms of an extra-statutory concession to remove some of the "unintended results" of this decision. It is interesting to see how much can be discovered about this decision using the various sources generally available as at December 1989.

## Tracing a report of Zim Properties

This case is widely reported:

- 58 TC 371;

- [1985] STC 90;

- [1985] BTC 42;

- 129 SJ 68;

- (1985) 82 L S G 124;

- *Times* 19 November 1984.

There are also digests in: *Current Law Yearbook* 1984, para 268; 1985, para 237 and *Halsbury's Laws of England: Annual Abridgment* 1984, para 249

No single source will retrieve all of this information. Only LAWTEL and the CCH Editions looseleaf encyclopaedia, *British Tax Reporter*, acknowledge the report in *British Tax Cases*. LAWTEL records no other, but from the pages of the CCH encyclopaedia it is possible to find the citations for: *Simon's Tax Cases* - in the index and the citation for the *Reports of Tax Cases* - buried in a quotation from the Inland Revenue press release.

It was possible to trace the case by subject in LAWTEL, but it was necessary to take the following route to get to it:

Capital Gains Tax
  Compromising law suit
        Settlement sum a capital asset.

On the other hand, the table of cases in LAWTEL leads the user directly to the apropriate frame if the names of the parties are known.

*LEXIS* gives only TC and STC.

The *Current Law Case Citator* gives TC, [date incorrect] STC, SJ and LSG, as well as references to a couple of articles on the case. From the digest in the 1984 *Current Law Yearbook* it is possible to identify the report in *The Times* newspaper - but by no other means.

*Halsbury's Laws of England* gives STC, SJ and the digest in the *Annual Abridgement.*

References in *Legal Journals Index* cite the reports in TC and STC.

The Digest reveals nothing at all. Many examples of this kind would tend to undermine one's confidence in the work.

**Tracing the subsequent history of the decision**

The *Current Law Case Citator* gives no subsequent cases where the Zim decision has been noticed. A LEXIS search, on the other hand brings to light three cases:

Pennine Raceway Ltd v Kirklees Metropolitan Council;

Kirby (Inspector of Taxes) v Thorn EMI plc;

Donald Fisher (Ealing) Ltd v Spencer (Inspector of Taxes).

The results of the LEXIS search require some interpretation. For example, the Pennine Raceway decision is recorded twice, and there are various errors: Council is rendered as "CNUNCIL"; our case appears with "Poroperties" instead of Properties and the TC citation is given as 57 instead of 58. In the first two of these decisions Zim is applied, but in the third it is merely cited by Counsel in argument. With a database the size of LEXIS it is inevitable that there will be keying errors, and one is sometimes made acutely aware of the lack of editorial input.

A search on Profile, in the UKNEWS file, also reveals the Pennine Raceway decision.

The best source for most of the subsequent history of the decision is the *British Tax Reporter* which includes a discussion of the Pennine Raceway and Thorn EMI decisions as well as Zim. The Inland Revenue extra-statutory concession is also introduced in its proper context.

The information is harder to find in *Simon's Taxes* because one needs to consult the supplementary case index. The master case index has no entries for Zim.

It is possible to find the extra-statutory concession in *Simon's Tax Intelligence* but for that it would have been necessary to know firstly, that the document existed, and secondly, the date on which it had been published. As the publication of such documents is usually associated with an Inland Revenue press release, for more publications, one could have used the Hermes data base on Profile. However, the press release in question was issued before this file was established.

**Tracing journal comment**

The *Current Law Case Citator* reveals two articles - one each from the *Solicitor's Journal* and *Taxation*, but neither is sufficiently recent to mention the extra-statutory concession. *Legal Journals Index* reveals 12 articles and two case comments published in 1988 and 1989. All but one of these has been indexed under the heading "Capital Gains Tax" and all can be located from the case index.

## Conclusions

With this example, *Current Law* was the best source for tracing the various published reports of the case; LEXIS was best for identifying subsequent litigation where the case had been noticed; *Legal Journals Index* was the only source which listed all the recent journal comment. It is also clear that a looseleaf encyclopaedia was the best general starting point for someone who needed an overall introduction to the issues presented by this case, and the subsequent matters arising from the decision. But, to research the problem in depth, it was necessary to revert to the journal comment.

These are points which can only be established retrospectively. A different example would almost certainly have given rise to startlingly different results. Legal research problems have one thing in common: they are all different.

## APPENDIX 2 SPECIALIST REPORTS

This is a selection of some of the more commonly used specialist series of reports. The British & Irish Association of Law Librarians has recently published a bibliography of commonwealth law reports.

| | |
|---|---|
| **Administrative law:** | *Crown Office Digest.* |
| **Building and construction:** | *Building Law Reports; Construction Industry Law Letter; Construction Law Reports.* |
| **Company:** | *British Company Cases*; *Butterworths Company Law Cases;*, *Company Lawyer.* |
| **Criminal:** | *Criminal Appeal Reports*; *Criminal Appeal Reports (Sentencing)*; *Criminal Law Review.* |
| **Employment:** | *British Equal Opportunity Cases*; *Industrial Cases Reports;*, *Employment Law Cases*; *Industrial Relations Law Reports*; *IDS Brief*; *Industrial Law Journal.* |
| **Family:** | *Family Court Reporter*; *Family Law Reports*; *Family Law*; *Practitioners Child Law Bulletin.* |
| **Housing:** | *Housing Law Reports.* |
| **Immigration:** | *Immigration Appeals.* |
| **Insurance:** | *Lloyd's Law Reports*; *Insurance Law Monthly.* |
| **Intellectual property:** | *Fleet Street Reports*; *Reports of Patent Cases*; *European Intellectual Property Review*; *Intellectual Property for Business.* |
| **Litigation:** | *Litigation Letter*; *Professional Negligence.* |
| **Local government:** | *Local Government Reports; Local Government Review.* |
| **Magistrates:** | *Justice of the Peace Reports.* |
| **Personal injury:** | *Personal and Medical Injuries Law Letter.* |
| **Planning:** | *Planning Appeal Decisions; Planning Law Reports*; *Journal of Planning & Environment Law.* |
| **Property:** | *Property & Compensation Reports*; *Conveyancer and Property Lawyer*; *Estates Gazette*; *Rating and Valuation Reports; Commercial Leases.Estates Gazette Case Summaries.* |
| **Road traffic:** | *Road Traffic Reports*; *Wilkinson's Road Traffic Law Bulletin.* |
| **Taxation:** | *Reports of Tax Cases*; *Simon's Tax Cases*; *British Tax Reporter*; *British Tax Review*; *Tax Journal*; *Taxation*; *Tolley's Practical Tax.* |
| **Value Added Tax:** | *Value Added Tax Tribunal Reports; VAT Intelligence* |

Printed and published by
Legal Information Resources Ltd
Elphin House, 1 New Road, Mytholmroyd,
Hebden Bridge, West Yorkshire
HX7 5DZ

Tel: (0422) 886277
Fax: (0422) 886250
DX: 29584 Hebden Bridge